Y2K FAMILY SURVIVAL GUIDE

A Complete Action Manual
For Your Y2K Lifeboat

Avian M. Rogers

Foreword by
Leonard Nimoy

"Based on the results of the survey, I cannot be optimistic, and I'm genuinely concerned about the prospects of power shortages as a consequence of [Y2K] . . . I expect we will have brownouts and regional blackouts, and in some areas of the country there will be power failures . . . there is a 40 percent chance the power grid will go down."

— Senator Robert Bennett, (R-Utah) Year 2000 Committee Chairman (following a confidential survey of the nation's leading energy companies)

"There's no point in sugarcoating the problem. If we don't fix the century-date problem, we will have a situation scarier than the average disaster movie you might see on a Sunday night. Twenty-one months from now, there could be 90 million taxpayers who won't get their refunds, and 95% of the revenue stream of the United States could be jeopardized.

— Charles Rossotti, Commissioner of the IRS

"Experts who spoke at the Senate hearings believe that there may be localized disruptions. For example, in some areas, electrical power may be unavailable for some time. Manufacturing and production industries may be disrupted. Roads may be closed or gridlocked if traffic signals are disrupted. Electronic credit card transactions may not be processed. Telephone systems may not work.

— Excerpt from the Red Cross Web site re: Y2K

"Let's stop pretending that the Y2K isn't a major threat to our way of life. There is too much at stake for such uninformed wishful thinking. Perhaps, the time has come as though we are preparing for a war. This may seem extreme and unnecessary. However, if we prepare for plausible worst-case Y2K scenarios, then perhaps we can avoid at least some of them."

— Ed Yardeni, Chief Economist of Deutsche Bank Securities and international economic adviser on Y2K during keynote address to Bank for International Settlements April 1998

Published by Rutledge Hill Press, 211 Seventh Avenue North, Nashville, Tennessee 37219.

Distributed in Canada by H. B. Fenn & Company, Ltd., 34 Nixon Road, Bolton, Ontario L7E 1W2.

Distributed in Australia by The Five Mile Press Pty., Ltd., 22 Summit Road, Noble Park, Victoria 3174.

Distributed in New Zealand by Southern Publishers Group, 22 Burleigh Street, Grafton, Auckland, New Zealand.

Distributed in the United Kingdom by Verulam Publishing, Ltd., 152a Park Street Lane, Park Street, St. Albans, Hertfordshire AL2 2AU.

This book is intended as a general guide to preparation for potential disruption of services upon which the reader now depends. It is not intended, nor should it be considered, as medical, legal, financial or technological advice. For medical, legal, financial or technological advice or recommendations with respect to individual situations or concerns, please consult with an appropriate professional. The mention of specific products in this book does not constitute an endorsement by the publisher.

Library of Congress Cataloging-in-Publication Data

Rogers, Avian M.
   Y2K family survival guide : a complete action manual for your YK2
lifeboat / by Avian M. Rogers : foreword by Leonard Nimoy.
      p. cm.
   ISBN 1-55853-718-X
   1. Year 2000 date conversion (Computer systems)   2. Home economics
Handbooks,   manuals, etc.   I. Title.
QA76.76.S64R64   1999
005.1'5—dc21   99-30663
                                                            CIP

Printed in the United States of America

1 2 3 4 5 6 7 8 9—03 02 01 00 99

CONTENTS

Foreword   **vii**

Preface   **xi**

Acknowledgments   **xiii**

Introduction   **xv**

The Y2K Conundrum Hits Home   **xv**

No Silver Bullet but There is a Silver Lining   **xx**

How to Use This Manual—Keep It Simple   **xxi**

1. Food   **1**
   Food Storage Planning   **4**
   What Food to Store   **6**
   Proper Food Storage   **31**
   Kitchen Supplies and Equipment   **35**

2. Water   **38**
   Water Storage   **41**
   Water Treatment   **46**
   Water Sources   **59**

3. Power   **62**
   Energy Conservation   **69**
   Alternative Power Supplies   **72**
   Heating, Cooking, and Lighting   **86**

4. Health and Hygiene   **120**
   Advance Medical Planning   **122**
   Basic First Aid   **125**
   Vitamins and Herbs   **130**
   Personal and Family Hygiene   **136**
   Sanitation and Refuse   **138**

5. Money   **140**
   Documentation   **142**
   Money and the Post-Y2K Economy   **144**
   The Stock Market   **148**
   General Financial Preparedness   **153**

6. General Family Preparedness   **156**
   Transportation   **157**
   Communications   **159**
   Security   **160**
   Tools and Repair   **162**
   Family Entertainment   **162**
   Moving   **163**
   Working through the Kinks   **164**
   Talking to Your Children about Y2K   **164**

Checklists   **168**

Preparedness Suppliers   **182**

Appendix 1   **191**

Appendix 2   **193**

Index   **196**

FOREWORD

Flying from Los Angeles to New York—two of the greatest metropolises in the history of human civilization—I am reminded of the legendary Atlantis. Atlantis may have been the most advanced civilization on earth. However, because its technological innovations were too advanced for it citizen's judgment, they ended up destroying themselves. As legend has it, this ancient civilization vanished into the sea to be a lesson to us all.

Atlantis is mythical and ancient, but the Y2K problem is very real, and very near. Because of a programming oversight, we are facing a global problem in how computers will read the date in the year 2000. When we go into the next millennium many computer systems may fail, disrupting power supply, water and food delivery, satellite communications, health care, and transportation. This year 2000 (Y2K) problem reminds us of the fate of Atlantis. Have our own rapid technological innovations outpaced our ability to control and foresee their ultimate consequences?

In the dead of winter, a myriad of failures may occur around the world. Computer glitches could cause electricity to stop pulsing, which would cause elevators to stop, heaters to shut down, and communication to be silenced. Streetlights, stoplights, and lights in buildings may flicker out. Credit cards and ATMs may cease to function. Water delivery systems may not deliver water for cooking, drinking, or bathing. Hospitals, clinics, and pharmacies may be unable to provide proper medical care. Banks and stock markets may suffer as a result of corrupt electronic record-keeping systems and businesses that cannot function without electricity and communications.

Many people compare the Y2K problem with a hurricane. We can see it coming and know it's there, but we're not sure about the extent of damage it will cause. The Y2K problem will hit the world on the same day. Of the billions of microchips and lines of code, if only 10,000 failures occur, they will most likely have a domino effect that will bring chaos. Y2K-compliant systems may be affected by noncompliant systems. Seriously affected economies in one part of the world may impact healthy economies everywhere else.

Despite the gargantuan task of fixing all the computer systems and the possible consequences of the Y2K problem, there is hope. A number of vital government organizations, such as the Social Security Administration, have been working on the Y2K problem since the mid-1990s. The credit card companies became aware of potential problems early because year 2000 expiration dates provided an early warning system. As a result, they are well prepared. Some major banks, such as Chase Manhattan, have been working on the Y2K problem since the early 1990s. Macintosh computers have been Y2K compliant since the mid-1980s. President Clinton has appointed a special Y2K czar, John Koskinen, to oversee a nationwide campaign to review and resolve every aspect of the Y2K problem. In other words, even though our society has been slow to realize the full implications of the Y2K problem, it is now being addressed with fervor.

World leaders in government, spiritual, and corporate circles have found themselves in one of the greatest dilemmas facing humankind. The dilemma is not the Y2K problem itself, rather the dilemma is in deciding how to prepare for its consequences. There are self-proclaimed Y2K experts who are alarmists, telling us that Y2K is the end of the world. Then there are the skeptics who claim that Y2K is all hype and there's absolutely nothing to be concerned about. The reality is that there are no Y2K experts because nothing like this has ever occurred before. No one knows exactly what is going to happen. It is important for you to find a reasonable balance between those who call for extreme survival measures and those who advise no action at all. The best we can do is work together, to prepare as individuals, families, and communities.

Without a doubt, we are living in one of the greatest periods in human history. It is an exciting time to be alive. We are enjoying unbelievably rapid advancements in technology. In a way, we are all responsible for the Y2K problem. We have all benefited from the technologies that improve our lives. Therefore, we have encouraged competition and thus more advancement at all costs.

Whatever perils our human ambition and shortsightedness may have caused, our even more powerful human spirit will find a way to overcome them. Let us use the Y2K problem as an opportunity to reflect on where we are headed as a civilization. If the omission of two simple digits can have worldwide impact, we must ask ourselves—before we rush too far forward: "What are we doing with genetic engineering, cloning, bacteriological warfare, death ray technologies, and pollution of the planet? What can we do as the inheritors and caretakers of this world to protect our home, our island in space?"

The primary goal of this book is to help families across the world to prepare and work together regardless of what may occur as a result of the Y2K problem. Yet there exists, even in 1999, a general state of denial, complacency, or even apathy about both the reality and the potential affects of Y2K. Unless we appreciate what may occur, we may not be ready either individually or as a civilization. Therefore, the conscientious preparation of your family and community will be the first steps in the development of a deeper, more authentic, sense of community around the world.

Live long and prosper.

LEONARD NIMOY, May 1999

PREFACE

I first heard about Y2K when a friend met me at the airport. He was unusually late and noticeably agitated. Fumbling with my bags, I asked, "You seem upset, are you okay?" At that, he blurted out, "I can't remember when I've been so blown away. I've been in business meetings all day and am finally beginning to understand just how serious the Year 2000 computer problem is, and how it could foreseeably change life as we know it."

My first response was to try to calm him down, "Oh come on, a little computer chip can't be the breaking point of our whole society. I'm sure with all those smart computer people out there, it will get fixed. Besides, the government wouldn't let anything serious happen."

The following day my wall of resistance only grew stronger as my friend continued to talk about how Y2K could cause widespread breakdowns on every level of society. It sounded so crazy, so inconceivable, that it was difficult to take in. However, over the following months I started reading newspaper blurbs, congressional reports, and other information about Y2K. Eventually, I worked my way out of my own denial. After talking with several Y2K experts from the computer and business fields about how it was already too late to fix many computers, the scope of the problem hit me.

How many of us marvel at the dazzling new technological advances—fax machines, cars that talk, blazing computers, and e-mail—that swept into our daily lives. How many of us ask, "how far can this go, and where is it taking us anyway?" I've often wondered about the promise of better living through these technological advances. They're supposed to make our lives easier, however, now we're expected to get more stuff done in less time.

The growth of technology has been clearly outpacing our ability to fully understand it's strengths and weaknesses. Although with Y2K breakdowns, it may slow us all down, at least for a little while. We may have an opportunity to take a closer look at what science and technology offers up to the Altar of Commerce. For example, what are the implications of cloning? How about fertility drugs? We don't really question these things as possibly interrupting a natural order of life. We just gawk at what science can do amidst news reports of the latest quintuplets, and science just marches on. While Y2K may look like Pandora's box, we could end up the wiser for it.

While learning about Y2K, I experienced a roller-coaster of emotions. I've been astonished, afraid, angry, overwhelmed, and every now and then I momentarily fall back into doubt. Then, I began to take action. Personal emergency preparation for Y2K involves more than gathering up your favorite foods and filling water bottles, it requires an emotional and psychological adjustment process that doesn't happen overnight. It's important to expect that you and other family members will go through many different reactions to Y2K and the risks it poses. Learn to practice patience, you'll need it.

While no one can claim to know exactly what will happen on January 1, 2000, I am confident that after reading this book you will agree that there is sufficient reason to make the necessary preparations for yourself and your family. The practical options presented here make use of the latest in technology as well as time-tested lore for emergency preparedness.

If we exercise a little wisdom along the way, we'll truly be ready for anything.

Prepare well; live well.

AVIAN ROGERS
www.nimoy2k.com

ACKNOWLEDGMENTS

Y2K emergency preparedness involves many subjects including food supply, water supply, alternative energy, health care, and the economy. To come up with the most useful guide as possible, I had to turn to numerous experts as well as loving friends and family for support. I am deeply grateful to you all:

Leonard Nimoy, who made this book possible with his vision and commitment. Thanks for giving and caring so much.

Denis Korn, who is a legend in food preparedness. Food and philosophy is always fun with you. (I'm sorry I made you miss your dentist appointment.)

Will Hepburn, who handles more assets than I'll ever dream of. Thanks for your financial insight and never making me feel stupid.

John Mauldin, editor and author, you are Superman. How does such a busy man find time to do even more with such humor and warmth?

Richard Williams, whose knowledge of water purification was valuable to me. Thanks for keeping our airlines supplied with plenty of good drinking water.

Andy van Roon, whose unflagging commitment and calming support kept me and this project going.

Scott Taylor, thanks for being a tireless resource and friend.

Michael Rogers, my wonderful father, who painstakingly reviewed the manuscript with great gusto and care.

Francea Rogers, my mother, who is always prepared and never wavers in her support.

Danielle Green, who inspires me to reach beyond my self-imposed limitations and makes my life bigger and better by association.

In addition, there are those that jumped in when others might have said, "I'm too busy." I would like to thank those who cared enough to make this book as helpful and accurate as possible including Ed Yardeni, Chief Economist of Deutsche Bank Securities; Rick Cowles, who is working around the clock to track the status of Y2K and the power grid; Carole Munson and Dr. Joe & Betty Morrow, who have stepped out of the denial in the medical professional to help people deal with Y2K in a practical healing way.

Finally, thanks to my editors, Mike Towle and Geoff Stone for their unflinching attention.

INTRODUCTION

"I believe that severe disruptions will occur, and that they will last perhaps about a month. Additional problems, ranging from annoyances to more serious issues, will continue cropping up throughout 2000. This prediction might be optimistic; it assumes that people will have done what is necessary to minimize the number of single points of failure that could occur. Accomplishing that alone in the time remaining will require a Herculean effort unprecedented in the history of computers."

—Peter deJager

"Our government is not going to get all of its critical systems fixed in time for the century change. The evidence for this is overwhelming . . . even John Koskinen, chairman of the President's Council on Y2K, has publicly acknowledged that the time to begin Y2K remediation is past, and the time has come for crisis management and contingency planning."

—Senator Bennett

The Y2K Conundrum Hits Home

Who would have thought that because of computers we'd be sitting around our kitchen tables and living rooms discussing the potential breakdown of our society? It sounds ludicrous, right?

You can ignore it and put it off as hype, but the fact remains that Y2K could cause widespread disruptions, if not out-and-out failures on every level of society. Like it or not, we depend on computers for everything from taking a shower to transferring funds. Imagine the impact on your life if you didn't have a well-stocked grocery store down the street, gas at the pump, ATM machines, pension checks, heat and light, health care, or the telephone. If you were sick, your life might depend on them.

It's hard to imagine all the work that computers do. For most aspects of organized society they are behind the scenes. Our insatiable demand for the services that computer technology provides has spawned exponential growth of the computer and microchip industry. Many people make light of the complex dependencies we have on technology and want to minimize the potential impact of the "millennium bug," suggesting that computers are something like a hammer you can pick up and put down whenever you want: "Oh, the computers aren't working today. That's okay, we'll just use our yellow pads for a while." If it were only that simple. The more we learn about the Y2K problem and its complexity, the graver the situation appears. Only a small percentage of computers and chips needs to fail to create significant infrastructure problems.

The problem is that many of our computer systems, software, and embedded chips won't be able to compute the roll over from 1999 to 2000. Since most computers and computer chips are programmed with a two-digit date rather than a four-digit date, when the date reaches "00," screwy things will happen. It's easy to understand that 2000 is greater than 1999, but "00" is less than "99." Some computers will interpret "00" as 1900 and crash. Crashing is preferred to a computer that produces bad data. For instance, if a non-compliant computer that usually sends out a monthly pension check to a seventy-three-year-old man born in 1927 thinks its 1900, it would subtract his age making him minus twenty-seven years old. Most computers will eliminate the negative sign and assume the man is twenty-seven years old. Flattering maybe, but not helpful if the check never gets sent.

Since computers manage and regulate so much, the possibilities for failure seem endless. "It could affect power, phone service, air travel, and major governmental service," said President Clinton. When Tom Sandler, president of Samsonite Luggage, proudly flipped a switch at a distribution center to demonstrate their Y2K compliance, he could only stand by helplessly as a Y2K computer glitch had a domino effect scrambling the entire distribution system, which hampered sales and operations for months. The estimated cost to the company was $14 million. Ralph J. Szgenda, the chief information officer of General Motors, told *Fortune* magazine (April 27, 1998) that there are "catastrophic (Y2K) problems" in every GM plant. When a grocery chain was testing its computer equipment, the computer read the expiration dates wrong and discarded caseloads of food it thought had expired.

The tiny microprocessors, often referred to as embedded chips, pose a more crucial problem. They are installed in thousands of crucial systems, such as elevators, hospital equipment, pipelines, water treatment plants, and power utility companies. At a senate Y2K conference, Senator Bennett stated that 2 to 5 percent of these embedded chips are expected to fail—we just don't know which ones. Non-compliant chips look just the same as compliant ones, if they can be found at all.

How is it that the technological wizards of our time were so oblivious to what now appears so obvious? The original decision that set Y2K in motion was made in the 1960s. In order to economize on data-storage space programmers used a two-digit year instead of four digits. So when the dust settles, the blame will not be placed on the innovators but on the managers who were driven by the bottom line. Now, hundreds of thousands of programmers are working as fast as they can to fix the problem. For many businesses, governments, and services, there just isn't enough time.

It is important to stay informed about what business and governments are doing to solve this problem because it indicates the scale of the problem. Bruce Webster, chairman of the Washington, D.C. Year 2000 Group says, "What we've noticed is that the longer someone works on the Year 2000 problem and the more involved they get and the more research they do, the more concerned they become."

"Y2K is Worse Than Anyone Thought," reported *Business Week* magazine (December 14, 1998) on spiraling Y2K remediation budgets for businesses. For example, AT&T's initial budget of $300 million is now $900 million; General Motors' initial budget of $400 million is now over $800 million; Merrill Lynch's initial budget of $375 million is now $560 million; McDonald's initial budget of $8 million is now $30 million. Would businesses be spending these huge sums if Y2K wasn't a critical problem?

Claims of Y2K readiness should be taken with a grain of salt. To cite a recent example from *USA Today*, the Pentagon had to come clean when they admitted to falsifying readiness reports for Y2K compliance. They never conducted the required tests on three out of five "mission critical" computer systems. According to *Vanity Fair* magazine (January 1999), William Curtis of the Department of Defense said, "Anyone who dared report anything besides (compliance) . . . was worried, that's because we shot the messengers." How many other "messengers" are being ignored?

"Does it come as a surprise to you that the Pentagon on occasion fudges on the truth?," asks Senator Bennett as he drolly tries to allay the public's concerns, "(at least) there aren't as many people lying to us as there used to be."

It's not that the Pentagon or private companies won't fix their systems; it's just that you can't believe everything you hear about Y2K readiness. As some businesses and public utilities face the possibility that fixes may be harder than first thought, they are putting together contingency plans. Employees at Pacific Bell, California's largest phone conglomerate, has issued statements that no leave will be allowed between December 15, 1999 and January 15, 2000. General Motors, Ford Motor, Wells Fargo Bank and the Federal Reserve are making similar announcements. A seriously impaired infrastructure will create an irate public and an urgent need for emergency services. These companies, and others, anticipate that they'll need every able-bodied person to handle the problems.

There are people who call this TEOTWAWKI—"the-end-of-the-world as-we-know-it." Others say the whole thing is drummed up by extremist propagandists harping for God or profit. The truth probably lies somewhere between these two extremes.

The most confounding part about the entire Y2K issue is that even the experts don't know exactly what will happen. Who can say how billions of lines of code and computer chips will perform on January 1, 2000? Senator Christopher Dodd (D-Connecticut) said, "you wouldn't want to be in an elevator, in an airplane or in a hospital (on New Years Eve)." How do *you* heed the warnings? Do you ignore the signs and party all night, assuming someone will fix it, or do you prepare for the worst?

If you want to prepare, the time to do it is now! This does not mean you're an extremist, but rather that you've decided that it's better to be safe than sorry. You probably wouldn't get on an airplane if there was a 15 percent chance of it crashing, so do you really want to be caught off guard if there is a 15 percent chance of the power grid going down? Or how about food shortages? Wouldn't it be better to be prepared so you don't have to depend on the government food depot? If you knew you were going to be in a car accident, would you make sure you had insurance? Well, you know there are going to be problems as a result of Y2K, so don't you want to be prepared?

The best way to protect yourself in the event of Y2K infrastructure failures is by becoming as self-sufficient as you can. You might think of Y2K preparation as a little like camping in your home except you get to sleep in your own bed. It means you have to be prepared to meet your family's needs without any outside help. This means preparing to live without electricity, water, or health care. This is similar to preparing for disasters like earthquakes, hurricanes, or snowstorms. Y2K is just another storm brewing, but your efforts to prepare could be invaluable to you and your family. Many of us have never given much thought to disaster preparedness. It requires a bit of the old "frontier spirit." On the other hand, we can actually *benefit* from the technological advances in preparedness food and equipment of the last twenty-five years, like freeze-dried and dehydrated foods, wind-up flashlights, battery inverters, and solar energy products.

Depending on your particular situation, different options will fit better than others; it is up to you to decide what's best for you and your family. You'll find lots of valuable information on the latest supplies and equipment to enable you to make the most of your preparedness kit. Remember, you don't have to be a true believer to make preparations. Simply prepare for the worst and hope for the best.

No Silver Bullet but There Is a Silver Lining

When talking to friends, family, and associates, you may hear someone ask, "can't some of those brainy computer guys come up with something to fix the problem?" With all the incredible software being developed these days, it's not unreasonable. Unfortunately, there is no silver bullet. It's not that the problem in and of itself is complicated, it's just that there is too much to fix and not enough time to fix it.

There are many hidden lessons to be learned. (Isn't there with everything in life?) The Y2K crisis can be a blessing with the right attitude. We may learn to give more support to our families and friends, reach out to our communities, and rediscover the art of relationships. Without television, we might talk to each other more. Clearly, Y2K is a wake-up call to rethink the role of technology in our lives. Technology has given us a great deal, but it also impoverishes our resources. If the utility companies shut down, we may be forced to heal the planet by using cleaner alternatives like solar power or wind power. You could take this time to rediscover the wonder of books, the inspiration found in poetry, and the fun in games.

There is a fulfillment that comes from being part of a church, your neighborhood, your own family, Y2K community action groups, sports teams, social clubs, classes, or some other group that is bigger than yourself. We may reach out in ways we never have before. Also, we may see our material "needs" diminish as the cash flow slows. Who knows? Y2K could be a blessing in disguise. Be prepared for anything.

How to Use This Manual—Keep It Simple

"Well, it's clearly a global problem. I think its potentially going to effect virtually everyone in the world in one way or another so I think it's worth everybody's attention at this point," said the chairman of President Clinton's Y2K Task Force, John Koskinen. The purpose of this manual is to offer you and your family clear directions on how to prepare as effectively as possible for any potential short-term or long-term Y2K problems.

The goal of Y2K emergency preparedness is to become as self-reliant as possible. This requires that you have the resources in your home to live as independently as possible. This means having a supply of food and water, an alternate power source, first-aid kits, medical supplies, tools, alternate transportation, extensive records, and safe harbors for your money. With all the uncertainties that Y2K presents, think of your preparation efforts as a life insurance policy for yourself and your family.

Start by putting together a preparedness plan. Think through all the various personal needs of everyone in your family. If you have children, ask yourself what they may need to be comfortable, and keep yourself sane at the same time. Does anyone in your family have special health needs that require prescription drugs or other medical care? Of course, your climate and living situation will influence your choices, too. Read through all the options in each chapter before you make your final decision. For example, it may make sense to install a propane heater and use a propane gas stove. On the other hand, if you live in a warm climate like

Florida, you may forgo the heating unit and use a dual-fuel camping stove for cooking.

There are checklists on page 168 that are designed to help you organize your plans and purchases. You can assign tasks by making copies of the checklists and distributing them among your family. There is also a list of Preparedness Suppliers at the back of the book. These are professional emergency preparedness and self-sufficient living people who are Y2K savvy.

There are many Y2K Web sites out there, and some are listed at the back of the book. They are great resources for information and supplies. You'll find lots of articles on Y2K, some from the mainstream press and some from respected experts that didn't make it in the "news." It's valuable to learn as much as you can about Y2K in order to understand more about what may come. It's all too easy to fall into denial and complacency when it's crucial that you remain focused on getting prepared. Also, the more you know the better you can help friends and family recognize their own personal risks from the Y2K problems.

Since this problem is unprecedented, no one knows exactly what's going to happen. Therefore, you will have to decide how extensive you think Y2K problems will be and for how long to prepare. In my opinion, a minimum of four weeks is best. There are people preparing for months and even years. The decision is up to you. One thing is for sure, you can't prepare *after* the Year 2000 anymore than you can hang plywood over your windows while the hurricane is raising your roof. Y2K is causing unprecedented demand, and many food and equipment manufacturers are unable to keep up. One well-known food manufacturer, Alpine Aire, is projecting sales to increase from an average $2 million a year to well over $35 million. As of this writing, some food reserve suppliers are on three- to six-month back orders. Another supplier said that he has already sold all the propane refrigerators he can get his hands on. Don't wait until supplies are gone. No amount of money can change the future. Begin preparing now!

CHAPTER 1

FOOD

"Store what you eat and eat what you store."

—James Stevens, author of *Making the Best of Basics*

"Variety is the spice of life."

—Traditional saying

The once-gorgeous Christmas tree sits sadly in the corner, looking as forlorn as an Easter bunny in July. It's December 27, a Monday, and Friday is New Year's Eve. The newspapers and evening news shows are hitting all the high notes of the past century, elaborating on all the accomplishments of the last 100 years while anticipating the next. Beneath all the rambling documentary highlights, the buzz about Y2K is at full pitch. It's now a familiar conversation topic among friends and family. After last night's debate about what's going to happen during the change over to Y2K, it suddenly occurs to you that you haven't done anything to prepare yourself.

On Wednesday the night before the new year, you promised yourself you'd go to the store to pick up some extra supplies after work, just in case there's something to this Y2K stuff. When you turn down the street you can see the grocery store, and it is jammed full. Cars are lining up on the street just to get in the parking lot.

Inside the store, you notice the long lines down the aisles. People are standing with beleaguered faces waiting to pay for whatever they've been able to find on the shelves. When you pass the bottled water aisle and it's empty, you get a sickening feeling that this isn't a nightmare you can wake up from. Panic has set in everywhere, and you've missed the boat.

You turn down the row of soups and find a couple of lonely cans of chicken broth. You grab them as if your life depended on it. In the cereal section, a box of Cocoa Puffs is all that's left. "How long can you live on Cocoa Puffs?" you ask yourself. You do better in the frozen food section where the Lean Cuisines have been passed over in favor of food that will keep without refrigeration. But for you, frozen dinners will have to do while you live on the hope that what you've heard about Y2K is bogus. Right? *But is it?*

When you see the last bundle of firewood being picked up, you feel cold just watching the cart roll by. It hits you now like a blow to the stomach. You are going to the end of the line with scarcely any thing in hand and there's nowhere else to go. You realize you waited too late and can't do a thing about it now.

What Happened to the Food?

Food inventory and distribution is monitored by a long chain of computers. For example, when you buy a quart of milk, the grocery store computer tracks the sale and automatically sends an order to the main office. From there it's sent to the main distribution center. Then the order is forwarded to the wholesale supplier, who delivers it to the dairy manufacturer. The shipment is then tracked from the dairy plant to the trucking company for delivery to the retailer. All of this sending and tracking is done by computer. If one of these computers reads "00" when the date rolls over to the Year 2000, many computers will respond to that as an error code and simply eliminate the order. This could, in turn, make food limited and/or expensive, if it is available at all. It may not sound like a big deal to fix, unless it happens everywhere at the same time. Keep in mind, many grocery stores only have a three-day inventory on average.

If computer systems that track orders were the only problem with food distribution, then it would be easier to deal with. But there are many other factors that could contribute to breakdowns in food supply. Some of these include failures of embedded chips in food processing plants, irrigation systems, and storage facilities. There have already been problems where hundreds of pounds of food were thrown away because the computer thought it was expired. Food production and delivery could also be hit hard in the event of power outages. Trucks and agricultural equipment might be unable to get fuel for operation, halting any kind of transport or production. Breakdowns in the railway system could also wreak havoc on food delivery.

In this country we've been fortunate and have come to take our food supply for granted. Food shortages could never happen to us. But you don't need to look any further than Russia with its massive food lines and the Black Market that people rely on for their sustenance to see how food shortages can indeed happen as a result of economic, political, and/or technological breakdowns. Anyone who lived through the Great Depression has firsthand experience of what food shortages were like in this country.

Why be a part of the crowd that is dependent on what the government can provide in a crisis? You'll add less demand to the system and be in a better position to help your family and support your community if you plan ahead and prepare for shortages. The mere *anticipation* of Y2K-related shortages could cause raids on supermarkets. With advance preparation, you will have more control; buy what you want, eat what you buy. Besides, do you really want to stand in anymore lines?

Even organizations like the Red Cross and the U.S. Senate Y2K Task Force (*Senate Report*, March 2, 1999) are getting more proactive in their messages to the public and recommend that food be stored in case supply and delivery problems occur.

Food is often the first thing people think of when preparing for
any type of emergency, whether it's Y2K, a hurricane, or a snow-
storm.

Here's what we'll cover in this chapter:

> **A. Food Storage Planning**
> **B. What Food to Store**
> **C. Proper Food Storage**
> **D. Kitchen Supplies and Equipment**

A. Food Storage Planning

Planning is important when storing food. Before you start hap-
hazardly buying items off store shelves and stuffing them indis-
criminately into the kitchen, garage, or basement, you need to
develop a workable and affordable plan that will keep your family
happy and healthy while minimizing effort and food waste.

Food presents the toughest preparedness challenge because
what we *like* to eat and what we *need* to eat to stay healthy depends on so many differences in individual tastes, lifestyles, and
health needs. Another thing to consider is how *long* you want to
prepare for. Storing a two-week supply of food is very different
from storing food for six months.

It's impossible to predict exactly what will happen with Y2K,
but it is best to store enough food for at least two to four weeks.
Some people are stocking enough food for up to six months and
longer. This may sound like a mountain of food, but you'd be
amazed at how much food you can cram into a relatively small
space.

Think through your own personal preparedness timeline.
Even as services are restored in the days, weeks, and months
after January 1, 2000, and more food becomes available, shortages
could persist. Due to potential business failures because of computer problems, a global recession could well be the worst and

most long-term result of Y2K. Obviously, implementation of a good food storage plan is valuable protection from such an economic storm. While it may seem financially stressful now to have to buy a lot of food, you'll be grateful to be in good shape should serious food problems occur. Don't go into debt to store food, instead make financial sacrifices like spending less on going out to the movies, restaurants, or other extras, and stock up on a little at a time.

Y2K preparedness is a personal thing. Assess the risks yourself and determine what length of time you feel most comfortable preparing for. Self-sufficiency for the unknown is what preparedness is all about and should go a long way in a post-Y2K world.

Where Do I Start?

Like a hurricane, Y2K may appear to be a thousand miles offshore, too far away to do any damage. You can hope it veers away from your area, but as it gets closer and closer, you'll find yourself with fewer options as each day passes. However, if you plan ahead, you won't be grabbing whatever is left on grocery shelves.

Make planning an active process of working through all your family's various needs as realistically as possible. Get everyone in the family involved and cover all the bases—the length of time you're preparing for, number of people, what the kids like, and what cooking supplies you need. After reading through the chapter, fill out the checklists in the back of the book. (*See Food Storage Checklist and Kitchen Equipment and Supplies Checklist at the back of the book.*) The checklists are intended as a guide to help you begin planning. Write down the kinds of foods you eat or would buy for emergency preparedness (consider storability and nutritional content). You don't want to realize too late that you forgot an essential item because of poor planning. This initial planning process will most likely be revised as you think of more things to add to your list. However, the sooner you get things on paper, the sooner you'll have a plan.

Planning does not mean dilly-dallying with decisions. Begin to take action with your food storage plan immediately. Some food companies are already experiencing long delays in getting products out to their customers so it's essential that you start stocking up now.

B. What Food to Store

With the amazing variety of foods available today, it is easier to store food everyone will like. Although you can store foods you prefer, there will be some adjustments to the way you prepare your food. You probably won't be able to "pop" things in the microwave. It is important to keep in mind preparation methods when deciding what food to store.

# of people	Amount of food	# days	Total food
	_____		_____
	_____		_____
_____ X	_____ X	_____ =	_____

There are two main categories that your stored food will fall into:

1. **Off-the-shelf grocery food**
2. **Emergency preparedness food reserves:**

▸ **Freeze-dried**
▸ **Dehydrated foods**
▸ **MREs (Meals Ready to Eat)**

You may not use all of the different types of foods, but we'll go into each type in detail so you'll know a little bit more about them in order to decide what's best for you. You can pick and choose from these categories once you've completed the chapter and have had a chance to "digest" all the information.

The optimal food storage plan should incorporate a balance of foods that satisfy both short-term (quick and easy off-the-shelf items, MREs, or freeze-dried foods) and longer term (dehydrated foods, grains, and beans) needs. It is best to be prepared to handle whatever needs arise by factoring in quality, cost, ease of use, and familiarity into your food plan. It is also important to think about foods that require little or no preparation, like freeze-dried foods and MREs, since your options may be limited if the power goes out in your area.

Start to incorporate stored foods into your diet now. This will also help you determine what your family really will eat, so you don't end up with a bunch of stuff no one wants. The motto is: "Store what you eat and eat what you store." The bottom line of your stored food plan is to buy items that store well without refrigeration.

Y2K Preparedness Foods Comparison Chart

This chart is merely a summation of the various preparedness food options. Please review the section on each food type for a more detailed explanation.

Type of Foods	Familiarity	Cost	Ease of Preparation	Long-term Storage	Availability
Off-the-Shelf Groceries (Non-Perishables) including canned, boxed, and bagged goods.	familiar foods that the family is used to	routine	easy to prepare the foods you make every day—Soups, cereals, tuna, peanut butter, snacks, etc.	6 mos.- 2 yrs., depending on item. (not meant for long-term storage)	readily available at grocery stores, until any last minute rush
Bulk Foods	not as familiar as pre-packaged food as these are in their raw form	very inexpensive	can be long preparation and cooking times	with proper storage it will store for long term. Wheat stores a very long time, brown rice only about a year	suppliers are often in out-of-the-way places, and you must package the food yourself
Freeze-dried Foods	familiar ready-made entrees	reasonable but 50% to 100% more than dehydrated	quick and easy, just add hot water	will last many years, if stored in cool, dark, dry place	expensive if purchased in camping stores, must be ordered from food reserve company for the best prices

Type of Foods	Familiarity	Cost	Ease of Preparation	Long-term Storage	Availability
Dehydrated Foods	requires getting used to less familiar foods, learning new recipes	very inexpensive	can be long preparation and cooking times	will last many years, if stored in cool, dark, dry place	make at home with a dehydrator or can be ordered from a food reserve company
MREs—Meals Ready to Eat	new to most people	reasonable $5 to $6 per meal	instant, can be heated or eaten as is	will last many years, if stored in cool, dark, dry place	can be found at some surplus store, otherwise must be ordered from food reserve company

1. Off-the-Shelf Grocery Food   These are the nonperishable foods that you buy every day at the grocery store or at the warehouse stores like Sam's Club or Costco. Here is a list of the most common categories:

a. **Canned food**
b. **Dry food**
c. **Grains and beans**
d. **Cooking essentials and condiments**
e. **Snacks and treats**
f. **Special needs**
g. **Bulk foods**
h. **Pet foods**

Much of the nonrefrigerated food that we buy at the grocery store has a shelf life of six months to two years, so storing the things you're used to is fine. If you have a week's worth of food at home, pick up several more cans, boxes, and bags of whatever your family likes on your trips to the grocery store, thereby increasing your supply every week. If you like tuna, just buy more of it. Be sure to read the expiration dates of everything you buy. Unfortunately, some manufacturers print their expirations in code so you can't determine dates unless you call them. Generally, cans will last for at least one year without losing nutritional content. (For more information on stored foods call or write the USDA/Utah State University Extension Service, 435-797-2200; 4900 University Boulevard, Logan, UT 84322.) To store foods that expire in six months or less, buy them closer to the new year so they'll last into 2000. However, don't wait until December to *begin* buying food; supplies could already be limited by then! (*See the Food Storage Checklist at the back of the book to help you organize your own shopping list.*)

As you build up your inventory, regardless of the types, you always want to rotate your foods so you are using those you bought earliest. The best way to keep track is to mark and date your food according to the use-by date, *not* the date you purchased it because different types of foods have different use-by dates. This way you always know that your foods are providing you with the best nutrition and taste possible. For this reason, avoid buying more foods than you can use within the storable period. This is where good planning comes in. As preparedness expert James Stevens says, "Use it, or lose it." So rotate, rotate, rotate.

a. Canned Goods Regular canned foods like tuna, soups, fruit, and vegetables are fine for food storage for the period the manufacturer indicates on the can, usually one to two years, except canned citrus foods and juices, which have a shorter shelf life of between six to eight months. Of course, if a can shows signs of "bulging" discard it immediately. Canned goods typically have a longer shelf life than jars. Glass jars with foods like soup or applesauce tend to expire at around six months, although peanut butter is certainly an exception to that and will last up to two years.

Canned foods are also good because they don't require cooking, although you may want to heat some. For bulk canned goods (#10 cans) you can go to a reputable food reserve company that uses the latest in canning technologies that deoxygenate the food in airtight durable cans. These techniques can dramatically increase the storage time of many foods to five years and even longer. Call Essentials 2000 or Millennium III Foods for these types of foods. (*See page 182 for phone numbers.*)

#10 can

Courtesy of Major Surplus and Supply

b. Dry Foods Add dry packaged foods and mixes to your list like cold cereals, macaroni and cheese, oatmeal, and other foods that you normally use. Cereals and pastas are packaged to have a shelf life of about six months. After that time, they begin to lose taste and become either stale or, in the case of pastas, harder to reconstitute.

Other nonperishable foods to store include grains like wheat (or flour), beans and lentils (legumes), crackers, bouillon cubes, fruit bars, granola bars, peanut butter, dried fruits, jerky, trail mix, tea bags, and coffee. Instant rice and potatoes store well, too.

Powdered milk is an important part of any food storage plan and can be picked up at the grocery store. However, because it is so susceptible to moisture, it is best to purchase it in professionally sealed cans from a food reserve supplier. (*See Preparedness Superstores at the back of the book*.)

Powdered Milk Tip: Add a few drops of vanilla extract and aerate the powdered milk to get the best flavor.

c. Beans and Grains   For health's sake, let's take a closer look at some important staples like beans and grains that should be included in any *long-term* food storage plan. Legumes, like lentils and beans, are an excellent source of protein, especially when combined with a grain, as in lentil soup with rice or chili and corn bread. Scientists recently found that legumes help stabilize blood sugar levels, balance insulin levels for hours and metabolize fat. The Harvard University School of Public Health reported that legumes may also be a strong defense against certain cancers. So, think *healthful* as you inventory food!

Focus your purchases on small grains and beans since they cook faster and therefore consume less water and fuel. Garbanzo beans, for example, take a long time to cook, but lentils are small so they cook much faster. Millet is another excellent fast-cooking grain. (Health food stores carry millet.)

Millet Tip: Put a cup of dry millet in a thermos, fill with hot water. The next morning add raisins or other dried fruit for a tasty breakfast of hot cereal. Try other grains, too, like oats.

Brown rice is fine for short-term storage and good to have around because of its high nutritional content, but it does not store well long-term because of its natural oils. It is highly vulnerable to rancidity after a year. For best long-term results, store the "instant" type white rice. This kind of rice is not as nutritious as brown rice but will keep longer.

It's no great mystery why wheat has been used for eons. It stores for years if properly preserved in its whole grain form, it's economical, and it is very diverse. The "red" or hard wheat has a higher nutritional content than the pastry type and stores longer. However, some people have a wheat/gluten intolerance so not everyone can eat it, especially every day.

Some simple uses for wheat:

- As flour for baking pancakes, breads, and muffins
- Whole-grain cereal (cooked as is)
- For sprouting (in salads and sandwiches, or eaten as is)

Sprouting: Sprouting is an excellent way to generate a fresh and nutritious produce that contains many essential vitamins and minerals. To spice up your diet of canned meats and grains, toss the sprouts with a little olive oil and vinegar, throw in some nuts and freeze-dried vegetables, and voilà! You have a fresh salad.

Just about any whole grain or seed can be sprouted. Alfalfa beans, mung beans, clover and radish seeds are easily accessible for sprouting. It may be a good idea to get beans or seeds that work well with either cooking or sprouting, like whole lentils or sunflower seeds. Be sure to get nonhybrid seeds as they will produce new seeds that can be planted or sprouted. You can purchase a sprouting kit through health food stores or emergency preparedness suppliers and some include seed packs.

Most of us eat a lot of flour products such as breads, pastries, cereal, and even sauces and soups. Be aware that the flour you buy in the store in bags is loaded with moisture so it doesn't keep well; it's fine for a few months. For storage of flour beyond a year or more, it's best to purchase wheat as a whole grain in bulk, and then make it into flour as needed with a grain mill. Cornmeal is another excellent grain for food storage. You can make tortillas or cornbread out of it, and eaten in combination with beans and rice, you have a complete protein meal that everyone will like. To find whole grain in bulk look in the Yellow Pages under "Commodity Brokers," "Grain Brokers," or "Food Brokers."

d. Cooking Essentials and Condiments Whatever you do don't forget essentials like cooking oils, onions, bouillon, baking power, vanilla extract, powdered margarine, vinegar, soda, yeast, powdered milk, and tomatoes. Without them, you'll be out of luck with many of the most basic recipes. Though they may not sound too good, include powdered eggs on your list as they are a complete protein and a fine substitute for any recipe that calls for regular eggs.

Crisco (HVO: hydrogenated vegetable oil) will store for extended periods of time at room temperature. This is an easy way to store cooking fat for a long time, but since it is not the most healthy choice, you should keep it out of your regular food rotation, using it on rare occasions.

Some foods like mayonnaise or salad dressing will store without refrigeration as long as the bottles are unopened. If these are things you like, you can buy small jars that you can use up quickly. Good taste goes a long way when operating in a disaster mode so, stock up on lots of spices, too! It's one thing to have to deal with some inconveniences but who wants to eat lousy food?

e. Snacks and Treats To keep everyone's spirits up, be sure to get some of your favorite snacks and treats, like chips, cookies, and candy. Comfort foods are important in times of stress and help everyone stay on an even keel by reducing tension. Mix up the menus! Unless you can swallow macaroni and cheese every night, it's good to have a variety of foods for two months rather than a year's worth of wheat and beans.

f. Special Needs   Keep in mind any special dietary needs such as food for infants or the elderly. In the case of babies, have plenty of infant formula on hand. Also, canned dietetic foods, juices, and soups may be helpful for the ill and elderly. Keep an extra supply of multivitamins and other nutritional supplements around for everyone. (*See the Herbal Health Kit table on page 134.*) Talk to your doctor or pediatrician about what additional nutritional requirements might be anticipated in order to prepare in advance.

Emergency Baby Formula: Single Serving—1 1/3 cups boiling water, 1/3 cup plus 2 tablespoons powdered milk, 1 tablespoon vegetable oil, 2 teaspoons sugar/syrup, 1/9 crushed multivitamin. Per Day—4 cups boiled water, 1 cup plus 2 tablespoons powdered milk, 3 tablespoons vegetable oil, 2 tablespoons sugar/syrup, 1/3 crushed multivitamin. Check with pediatrician before using this formula.

g. Bulk Foods   When talking about storing foods, the option of buying foods in bulk comes up. Typically, these are things like wheat, rice, beans, and sugar that can be purchased in large sacks or bags at very low cost and thus, extend your budget beyond what you might have thought possible. As with most things in life, the more you're willing to do yourself, the more money you save.

The warehouse wholesalers like Costco or Sam's Club sometimes carry larger containers of staples like rice, but their inventory is often limited on these kinds of foods. For the best deals and better selection, you'll have to research what's available in your area. Look in the Yellow Pages under "Restaurant Supplies" and/or "Feed-Wholesale and Manufacturers," and call for prices. For example, whole unground wheat is amazingly cheap right now—fifty pounds for two to three dollars.

To give you more of an idea of costs, the following are examples of prices at the time of this printing from a local restaurant supplier:

Food	Size	Price
Rice		
Instant	25-lb/50-lb bag	$16/$30
Brown	25-lb bag	$11
Sugar	25-lb bag	$20
Lentils	25-lb bag	$10
Bulgur	25-lb bag	$36

h. Pets (Don't forget them!) Whatever you do, don't forget to stock up on pet food! After all, our pets are completely dependent on us. Consider that in a time of disaster, pet food may be low on the list of those in charge of emergency supplies. It's wise to begin stockpiling at least six to twelve months of food.

The sacks that dry pet food come in are not ideal for long-term storage, but if you place the food in large plastic containers in a cool, dry place, it should be fine. In the case of canned food, buy it in bulk to save money, and store it in a cool place. Just like our food, be sure to pay attention to the expiration date on pet food and rotate it.

For your feline friends, don't forget to pick up an ample supply of kitty litter. Make sure it's the same brand they're used to. Some cats will rebel if you change brands on them and decide that the living room carpet is better. Also, pick up extra flea collars and any special medications.

If you have other kinds of pets, stock up on extra supplies for them, too.

2. Emergency Preparedness Food Reserves   As January 1, 2000 draws near you may become more concerned. If you think the Y2K crisis will cause serious food shortages, you may want to purchase dehydrated, freeze-dried, or professionally canned food from a professional food reserve company. These are foods that have been packaged using special techniques to preserve the foods for long-term storage. Usually these types of foods include fruits and vegetables, meats and meat substitutes, powdered milk, and cheese. These items typically come in a large #10 can (i.e. canned corn, apple flakes, dehydrated potato flakes, etc.) or specially sealed pouches so you can also purchase these foods à la carte. To make it easier on the customer, many food reserve companies organize a variety of items into complete food kits and sell them as a one-year supply for one person that can be divided among family members to fit whatever timeline you want. For example, if you have four people in your family, a one-year kit would last roughly three months. For eight people, you may choose to get two one-year kits.

These foods are designed for long-term storage, but another benefit of purchasing a long-term food storage kit is that the food reserve companies take the guesswork out of the nutritional content of your meals. By purchasing a long-term food storage kit, you can be sure that you're getting the proper amounts of protein, carbohydrates, fiber, vitamins, and minerals. Depending on the company, these kits usually consist of a combination of dehydrated food and bulk staples. The higher quality (and higher priced) food kits also include freeze-dried foods.

These long-term food storage kits may seem expensive, but compared to typical consumer food prices in the supermarket, these packages can actually be far less per serving, particularly with the dehydrated foods. If you're not used to buying these large quantities, who knows, you may learn to like the savings!

Sample Food Reserve Cost from Millennium III Dehydrated Foods

One-Year Kit (Dehydrated Food Package* includes protein, fruit, vegetable, and dessert)$1595

Meal Cost Breakdown

per meal	$1.50
per day	X 3
Total per day	$4.50

*This example is their lowest cost package. The food reserve companies are very knowledgeable about Y2K and happy to help you. Contact the food suppliers directly. (*See Preparedness Suppliers on page 182 for more information about their products and package deals.*)

A little note: Many of the food reserve supply companies are already inundated with orders due to Y2K concerns. Be prepared to wait for up to six to eight weeks for delivery and it could be more! You'll also have to pay up front.

Let's look at the differences between a) freeze-dried, b) dehydrated foods, and c) MREs (Meals Ready To Eat) so that you'll be more qualified to select what works best for you.

a. Freeze-dried Foods Freeze drying is the ultimate technology for preserving food. The process is the best at retaining the integrity of the food for long-term storage. It can be prepared quickly by just adding hot water. This is ideal since cooking capabilities may be limited and fuel must be rationed. A major selling point of freeze-dried foods is that these foods can be purchased as ready-to-eat entrees like Chicken Primavera, Beef Rotini, or Teriyaki Turkey. They reconstitute very quickly, so they take very little energy to prepare.

As the preferred method of food processing (when compared to dehydrating food), freeze drying does not damage the nutritional content of the food and maintains the flavors and seasoning most closely to when the food was originally prepared. Freeze drying works especially well for meats (meats do not work with regular dehydration methods) and is also excellent for any other type of food including fruits, seafood, pastas, vegetables, and eggs. Freeze-dried foods can even be eaten as is, without reconstituting. The fruits are particularly tasty this way.

Freeze drying isn't something you do at home, since the process requires expensive and unique manufacturing equipment. Freeze-dried foods are higher quality than dehydrated, but you'll pay about 50 to 100 percent more per meal. Also, you need to make sure to keep opened cans or bags well sealed once opened to reduce the food's exposure to moisture.

Sample Costs of Freeze-dried Foods

Mountain Chili (Serves 2)	$5.50
Chicken Primavera (Serves 2)	$6.50
Teriyaki Turkey (Serves 2)	$6.25
Teriyaki Turkey (#10 cans, 12 Servings)	$25
Beef Stroganoff (#10 cans, 12 Servings)	$23
Soup-Minestrone (#10 cans, 12 Servings)	$22
Corn (#10 cans)	$27
Peas (#10 cans)	$22
Peaches, Diced (#2.5 can)	$7

Advantages:

- They have up to a twenty-year shelf life.
- They retain the original taste and nutritional value of the food.
- They are quick and easy to reconstitute, requiring little fuel and water reserves.
- No preservatives are necessary.
- They are super-lightweight and compact product.
- There are a wide variety of freeze-dried foods available.

Disadvantages:

- They cost more, especially compared to dehydrated food (50 to 100 percent more than dehydrated per meal).

b. Dehydrated Foods   First, let's not get dehydrated foods mixed up with items you might dehydrate in your own home dehydrator. These are emergency reserve dehydrated foods here that use the latest technologies to dehydrate and specially package these foods for a long-term shelf life of up to twenty years. Dehydrated foods will give you the biggest bang for your emergency food buck. You can eat cheaper, longer with dehydrated food than any other available.

Dehydrated foods come in a wide variety. Some foods that dehydrate particularly well include: onions, mushrooms, potatoes (flakes, granules, dices), corn, bell peppers, applesauce, tomatoes, and carrots. Also, professionally dehydrated milk in #10 cans will store longer and taste better than what you get at the store. One of our favorite dehydrated foods is TVP (textured vegetable protein). It comes in several flavors like beef, chicken, and taco. Because it is made from soy, it is an excellent source of protein. Beans and peas don't hold up so well when dehydrated.

Make sure you have a couple of cookbooks on hand that show you how to prepare dehydrated foods. The more comfortable you are preparing dehydrated foods, the better your food will taste. (*See Cookbooks for Stored Foods on page 186*. Some food reserve companies will throw in a cookbook with your food package.)

Tasty Tacos: Mix up some cheese sauce powder, some taco TVP, and some bottled salsa; pour over some chips or tortillas, and you've got some very tasty nachos or tacos.

Advantages:

- They provide an excellent value for your money.
- Dehydrated foods are usually packaged in large #10 cans using technology for extra long shelf life (five to ten years).
- It is easy to store large amounts in small spaces since the size and weight of the foods have been dramatically reduced by the removal of water.

Disadvantages:

- Loses taste, nutritional value and visual appeal over time
- Can be slow to reconstitute, and many require cooking for a longer period of time than freeze-dried foods.

    c. MREs MREs (Meals Ready to Eat) were developed by the U.S. military and are the quintessential emergency food source. They've come along way since the days of basic "K" or "C" rations, and MREs can be quite tasty. They are convenient to prepare and portable. Designed as a fully hydrated flexible package, MREs are handy to grab on the run. For example, if you had to walk a fair distance to go find water, you'd have a nutritious and easy-to-carry meal to bring with you. Also, if you were to run out of fuel for your stove, you're covered because MREs can be eaten cold. The only thing you need water for is to mix the powdered drink.

Despite all their benefits, you shouldn't make MREs your *only* food source in emergencies because they have a low fiber content. The best way to use them is to incorporate them with other foods over the course of a week and have them on hand for when you need something quick. It's recommended that you not eat MREs for more than seven days in a row or in great quantities over a thirty-day period.

MREs are typically sold by the case as twelve complete meals for around $60 to $65 per case. This includes the entree, crackers, dessert, chewing gum, spoon, napkin, and a drink. They even throw in Tabasco sauce!

MREs have a long shelf life: up to four years or more if stored at 70 degrees or about a year and a half if stored at 100 degrees.

MRE Shelf Life

84 months at 60 degrees
55 months at 70 degrees
48 months at 80 degrees
30 months at 90 degrees
18 months at 100 degrees
1 month at 120 degrees

Advantages:

- They are ready to eat and store for up to seven years.
- You don't have to rehydrate them.

Disadvantages:

- They are low in fiber.
- You have to order them from food reserve companies.

Food Preparedness Examples and Suggestions

This chart is meant to illustrate how different types of food can be incorporated into an overall emergency food preparedness time-line. You'll quickly see that the longer you plan to store food, the more sense it makes to add long-term food storage items to your plan. For a more detailed explanation on each type of food, review the section on each food type previously discussed.

Preparedness Time	Perishable Food (these are the foods you'll eat first)	Off-the-Shelf Food (most of these foods will last 6 to 18 months)	Quick Response Foods (these are emergency foods requiring little or no preparation)	Long-term Storage Foods (foods that can last 5 years or more)
First 72 Hours Jan. 1-3, '99	meat, fruits, vegetables, milk, and frozen foods that will thaw without refrigeration	cold cereal, pastas, oils, canned goods . . . some meals require cooking	freeze-dried foods or MREs, and dehydrated fruit and nut mixture	
1 Week	most perishable foods will soon run out or spoil: potatoes, onions, squashes, leeks, carrots, some fruit like apples will last longest	you can easily go a week on these foods; add canned meats and fish into diet (you may want to mix with quick response foods to ease the cooking burden during power outages)	freeze-dried foods or MREs, and dehydrated fruit and nut mixture	
1 Month	potatoes, onions, squashes, leeks, carrots, some fruit like apples will last longest (other perishables are gone)	can continue to use canned and dry foods (pay close attention to nutritional balance)	freeze-dried foods or MREs, and dehydrated fruit and nut mixture	freeze-dried food, MREs, dehydrated food, whole grains, and specially canned foods (dehydrated foods and grains require longer preparation times as compared to other foods)

Food Preparedness Time (*continued*)

Preparedness Time	Perishable Food (these are the foods you'll eat first)	Off-the-Shelf Food (most of these foods will last 6 to 18 months)	Quick Response Foods (these are emergency foods requiring little or no preparation)	Long-term Storage Foods (foods that can last 5 years or more)
3 Months	N/A	can continue to use canned and dry foods (pay close attention to nutritional balance)	freeze-dried foods or MREs, and dehydrated fruit and nut mixture	freeze-dried food, MREs, dehydrated food, whole grains, and specially canned foods (dehydrated foods and grains require longer preparation times as compared to other foods)
6 Months or more	N/A	can continue to use off-the-shelf foods, but things may begin to go stale, especially if care is not taken to seal things up between uses	freeze-dried foods or MREs, and dehydrated fruit and nut mixture	freeze-dried food, MREs, dehydrated food, whole grains, and specially canned foods (dehydrated foods and grains require longer preparation times as compared to other foods; if possible, add home garden foods to meals

There's no set formula about how much off-the-shelf food versus long-term foods you should use. The *longer* you want to store food, the more careful you must be to store food properly, whether you package your own bulk foods, live on canned goods and grains, or purchase professionally packaged dehydrated or freeze-dried foods. (*See Proper Food Storage 31.*) The central factor in any food storage plan is achieving a good nutritional balance of stored foods with a mix of protein, fats, carbohydrates, fiber, vitamins, and minerals. You could live on macaroni and cheese for a week if you had to, but a month? Sure, many of us can get away with a few days of poor nutrition, but after that you could be taking your chances with your family's health and well-being. Ultimately, the final choices you make still come down to what suits your family, your budget, and most significantly, the length of *time* you want to store food.

Let's break food planning down into four different time periods to review some key considerations and offer some recommendations:

ONE WEEK'S FOOD STORAGE

Things to consider:

- Food preparation capabilities could be limited if power is out, so even if you are just storing what you normally eat, lean toward things that are easy to prepare.
- Meats, frozen foods, and dairy products won't keep beyond three days unless they are kept chilled.

Good Food Preparedness:
Double the amount of nonperishable groceries you normally buy for a one-week period during the months and weeks *before* January 1, 2000. These are the everyday things like peanut butter, pastas, rice, cereals, nuts, canned vegetables and fruit, tuna, and

whatever else your family likes that doesn't require refrigeration. Also, add extra canned meats, soups, and powdered milk (or milk substitute). Stock up on fresh produce during the last couple of weeks of December 1999, especially on foods that last longer like apples, oranges, eggs, potatoes, onions, and leeks.

Optimum Emergency Food Preparedness:
An *ideal* emergency plan also includes a small amount of "quick-response" foods like some freeze-dried food pouches and/or MREs for when you need something quick or cooking is not possible. You can also make do with things like nutritional health bars (often referred to as "granola bars") that you can pick up at the grocery or health food store.

TWO WEEKS' FOOD STORAGE

Things to consider:

- Most or all fresh produce and dairy products will be gone within the first week.
- Begin incorporating dehydrated foods into your meal plan.

Good Food Preparedness:
For two weeks, most of your foods can come right off the shelf from the grocery store just like for a one-week plan. However, due to the lack of fresh foods, make sure to pay particular attention to substitute the following items for fresh foods:

Instant milk
Powdered eggs
Canned meat, fish, other protein
Canned vegetables and fruit

Optimum Emergency Food Preparedness:
Same recommendation as mentioned in "One Week's Food Storage"—some freeze-dried food and/or some MREs. In addition, it would be a good idea to purchase some powdered dairy products from a food reserve company, such as instant milk ($20), eggs ($26 for over 325 eggs), and cheese powder. These particular products are often better than what you can get in the grocery store and will keep far longer.

ONE MONTH'S FOOD STORAGE

Things to consider:

- You need to be prepared to live entirely on nonrefrigerated nutritional foods.
- Fuel for cookstoves could become limited.
- Ease of cooking should factor into your food selection by buying foods that are easy to prepare like stews, soups, and any other "one pot" or straight-out-of-the-can meals.

Good and Optimum Food Preparedness:
When you get into storing food for a month or more, you should fill your pantry with a selection of dehydrated or freeze-dried foods, or you could put your own foods together, item by item.

Most companies selling dehydrated or freeze-dried food kits have already done the work of nutritional planning. In the case of freeze-dried foods, they are easy to reconstitute, which in turn saves on fuel. Dehydrated foods provide good nutrition and will last many years. Be prepared for longer cooking times than with freeze-dried, though. If you are organizing your own foods from the grocery store and bulk food items from restaurant or grain suppliers, be sure to store foods that are nutritionally balanced. You should include canned meats, fish, fruits, vegetables, grains, and beans. Also, don't forget to include treats like candy, granola bars, cookies, and chips to keep everyone's spirits up. You'll also have to handle proper storage on your own since many of these foods are not specially packaged for long-term storage. This approach may take more effort, but it gives you more room to customize your food purchases as you wish.

THREE MONTHS' FOOD STORAGE

Things to consider: *See one-month considerations*
This amount of food is a fairly large upfront investment, so the best way to protect the investment is by purchasing dehydrated or freeze-dried foods. That way, should Y2K food shortages be brief, the food can still be stored for years afterward for any future emergency.

Good or Optimum Food Preparedness:
Same as one month, except you'll be storing enough quantities for three months. You should also consider a sprouting kit and sprouting seeds: bulk grains, beans, and wheat.

Thoughts on Gardening
Think of gardening as part of a long-term strategy. Obviously, you can't expect to feed yourself from a garden in the middle of winter, but over time, it can pay dividends with good planning.

With an emergency approach to gardening, the best kinds of things to plant are "whole plant foods." This means growing things that can be eaten in their entirety. Things like lettuce greens, carrots, and radishes where the leaves, stems, and roots could be consumed throughout their whole growing cycle. Plants like tomatoes, where only the fruit of the plant can be eaten, are not nearly as efficient since you can't eat the leaves. You probably don't want to do whole plants exclusively but it is something to be aware of.

An extensive discussion on gardening would make up an entire book. That said, there are numerous books on gardening that you can pick up at your local bookstore or preparedness supplier. Here are some good books to add to your preparedness library:

- *How to Grow More Vegetables, Fruits, Nuts, Berries, Grains and Other Crops (On Less Land Than You Ever Thought Possible)* by John Jeavons
- *Burpee : The Complete Vegetable & Herb Gardener : A Guide to Growing Your Garden Organically* by Karan Davis Cutler
- *Rodale's All-New Encyclopedia of Organic Gardening: The Indispensable Resource for Every Gardener* by Marshall Bradley

C. Proper Food Storage

Once you get all your food home, what do you do with it? Proper food storage is the ticket to maximizing its shelf life. For good emergency preparedness, whether it's Y2K-related or not, you have to assume that you won't have refrigeration.

The most important thing is that foods should be kept dry and cool at a temperature of 75 degrees Fahrenheit or less. Many foods can even be frozen without harm, like dried packaged foods, freeze-dried food, and MREs. Never store glass jars in freezing conditions as they will break. Also canned goods should not be frozen as the contents will expand, which can cause a rupture in the seal of the can.

There are five elements that can cause food to deteriorate, so you want to protect food from these enemies:

▸ **Temperature** Heat is the greatest enemy of food. Food should be stored in a cool area (75 degrees). MREs can better tolerate higher temperatures, but even they won't last nearly as long above 75 degrees.

▸ **Moisture** For bulk foods or products susceptible to moisture (powdered milk, eggs, sugar, and cheese powder), store in large plastic bins with tight lids and the drier the climate the better. For those living in hot and humid climates, moisture can be a real problem so keep food as cool as possible. To minimize exposure to moisture double package your foods.

▸ **Oxygen** It causes rancidity and oxidization. For storage against oxygen and moisture, plastic bags, containers, and buckets are okay for a few months to a year, but not longer than that. For longer-term storage, food containers should have the ability to hold the atmosphere with an airtight seal. Best containers are sealed metal cans, sealed foil bags, and sealed glass jars.

▸ **Light** Like oxygen, it causes foods to break down. It is best to store food in a dark area.

▸ **Infestation** Some bulk grains will come with some insect infestation straight from the farm including the eggs. The live insects can be frozen and sifted out. Freezing does not kill the eggs, but cooking will. Bay leaves and/or rosemary can be put in the grain containers to deter insects.

Most foods will store just fine in their own packaging for around six months to a year or two, particularly if you also put these foods in large Rubbermaid or Tupperware-type plastic containers with tight fitting lids.

For bulk food items, five-gallon plastic containers with screw-top lids are good since they're easy to work with and store a lot of food. Be sure to use the ones made of food grade plastic. These buckets can be purchased from the food reserve and emergency supply companies. (You might be able to pick some up from a local bakery or restaurant for free.) One thing to know about plastic, however, is that it is porous and will eventually absorb smells and moisture. Also, rodents can eat through plastic.

Dehydrated and freeze-dried foods are designed for long-term storage. These foods are lightweight and take up minimal space since the water has been taken out of them. Also, once a can of freeze-dried or dehydrated food has been open, it will last for several months if you keep the cans sealed with the plastic lids that come with them.

Most people don't think of food storage in terms of years, but if you want your foods to last longer than one or two years, then you'll have to make additional preparations. It depends on how far you want to go. The only *true* long-term barriers against moisture and oxygen are metal and glass. These kinds of containers are typically professionally sealed with oxygen absorbers used to draw out the oxygen and extend the life of the food by suppressing rancidity and exposure to moisture.

To get the most out of your food budget, you can pool resources with friends and purchase large quantities of grains or dehydrated foods that you then divvy up. Consider purchasing an Impulse Sealer which enables you to do your own industrial quality food sealing in foil/ polyethylene laminate pouches of various sizes. Since they're foil (metal) bags, foods could last for five years and more. (Contact Essentials 2000 for more information about this do-it-yourself approach to food storage: 800-775-1991. They can also provide oxygen absorbers.) The sealer with bags and oxygen absorbers runs about $400, so it really makes sense to go in with a group of people to spread the cost around.

People often make the mistake of using Mylar bags for long-term storage, but because they are plastic, the shelf life for Mylar is one to three years. This is okay; it's just important to know the limitations.

Store Foods Where You Live

Regardless of the foods you choose, it's important to store your food where you can see it and access it readily. That means in the kitchen, or as close as possible. You might think that storing a pile of food means kicking the kids out of their bedroom to make room, but you'd be surprised at how much food can be stored in an average kitchen pantry. The point is that food should be stored where you live. That way it's more protected and easier to incorporate into every meal and make food rotation part of your daily food planning. There is a danger of wasting valuable food because people simply fail to use it in time. This is especially true when food is stored in a remote part of the house or down in the dark basement!

The basement may not be good for canned foods and other off-the-shelf items that you can incorporate into you daily meals. But for MREs, dehydrated foods, or bulk foods (grains or #10 cans) that keep for years, the basement or garage is a good place. Make sure they are in a dry place and packaged in a way that rodents can't get to them. You should fill up your kitchen pantry with off-the-shelf items before storing them in out-of-the-way places, like the basement or garage.

Begin to incorporate whatever foods you have decided to include in your preparedness plans now. This will help you see what rotates quickly and what is not moving through your inventory. Another thing, seal up the packages, boxes or cans of whatever food you've opened to keep it fresh as long as possible. Put your ravenous beastly ways aside and open packages and containers carefully so food can be easily re-sealed and you keep your food from going stale prematurely. It may not be so easy to just go down to the store and get more. Crackers, cereals, cookies, and breads should be kept in plastic bags, then in tight containers.

General Storage Tips:

- Foods should be stored in a dark, dry, cool place. Freezing is okay for freeze-dried, dehydrated, and dry foods but glass jars and wet-packed cans should not be frozen.
- Keep food sealed at all times.

- Open food containers carefully so that you can close them tightly after each use.
- Crackers, cereals, cookies, and breads should be kept in plastic bags, then in tight-sealing containers.
- Store packages of sugar, dried fruits, and nuts in screw-top glass jars or airtight cans to protect them from pests.
- For best storage results, double-seal boxed and paper-packaged foods like breakfast cereals, pastas, cornmeal, etc., in sealed plastic buckets or metal cans (i.e., garbage cans).
- Inspect canned foods for signs of spoilage before using.
- Rotate and date your food supply. Inspect your food periodically.

Most Common Mistakes with Food and Food Storage:

- Storing the kinds of food no one will eat unless on the verge of starvation.
- Not knowing how to cook with stored foods, especially dehydrated food.
- Not rotating foods regularly by storing too far out of sight and out of reach.
- Improper food storage—foods exposed to too much heat, light, moisture, air, or infestation.

D. Kitchen Supplies and Equipment

It takes more than food to supply yourself with everything you need to make meal preparation run as smoothly as possible. Evaluate the cookware you have. With cooking facilities limited during power outages, meals will have to be cooked in one or two pots that everyone dips into. Do you have large pots to cook for larger groups? How about big spoons, plates, cups, knives? Paper plates and plastic utensils and cups will take the stress out of cleaning up after meals when hot water is limited, but will increase the amount of trash. Also, keep tin foil around to reduce the amount of dirty pans to clean.

For food such as beans, grains, and other dehydrated foods, which can be slow to prepare, get a pressure cooker. This helps reduce cooking time significantly and thus saves precious water and fuel.

Various sizes of plastic bags will certainly be needed to store and protect food. Also, don't forget all the paper products that are good to have around: paper towels, napkins, coffee filters.

There are numerous items so carefully go over the *Kitchen Equipment and Supplies Checklist on page 172* to see what you have and bring it along to your favorite stores to fill in the rest.

Optional Appliances

For those of you ambitious types, there are a couple less common appliances you may want to get, especially if you want to store foods for longer term than one to three months. They are a food dehydrator and a grain mill.

Food Dehydrator

Dehydrators provide an excellent way to expand your stored foods and make the most of your budget! If you dehydrate fruits and vegetables through the summer and fall, you can store them through the winter and beyond. Dehydrated food retains the nutritional content while only removing the water. You can even make your own jerky without all the chemical

Courtesy of Food Pantrie Artwork

Dehydrator

preservatives. Food dehydrators are fairly inexpensive, at around $50, and they come with a recipe booklet to get you started.

Grain Mills

If you have an ample supply of bulk whole grains like wheat, you'll need to have a grinder on hand to turn that raw grain into flour to bake with. Obviously, you need to get one that can operate manually. Many electric grinders will convert to manual but be sure to check before you make a purchase. The metal burrs are more versatile for corn, oats, barley, soy, seeds and more since they don't get gummed up. However, some people prefer stone burrs for wheat (You've heard of stone-ground wheat.). There are mills with interchangeable burrs for greater versatility.

Photo by Brian Morris

Courtesy of Nazko

As the momentum for Y2K preparedness builds, mills are getting harder and harder to find so, pick one up quickly. Jade Mountain carries an excellent high performance grain mill with stone and iron burrs for around $140. (*See page 184 for their address and phone number*.) The Family Grain Mill (800-837-5162) has also been recommended and comes either as a hand-cranked unit or with a motor.

CHAPTER 2

WATER

I t's early on Saturday morning, January 1, 2000, and you've just awakened from a fitful sleep. You took it sort of easy at the New Year's Eve party last night, but that third glass of champagne that put you to sleep at around 12:30 has now awakened you. You're not sure what time it is because the digital light display on your clock radio is blank. You figure it's got to be around 5 or 6 A.M. because the bedroom is still dark, yet you know you've been asleep for several hours. The headache isn't so bad, but there's a touch of nausea in the pit of your stomach and you've got a wicked case of cottonmouth.

As you yank the covers off, you feel a room chillier than usual as you swing your legs over the side of the bed to get up. You stumble into the bathroom, grab the water glass you keep there, and reach inside the medicine cabinet for the packet of stomach fizzies. You pull the packet down and then reach over to turn on the water to fill the glass. The water comes on full for a few seconds before it suddenly gurgles a bit, then sputters out a few drops into your glass, certainly not enough to fill it halfway or even a third of the way to dissolve your tablets. You'd settle for a drink of plain water at this point, at least to get rid of the cottonmouth. But forget it, the well has run dry.

"Great," you think to yourself in your blurry state of consciousness. "I feel like yesterday's lettuce, and just my luck for the water to go out. Maybe I'd better call the twenty-four hour hotline or whatever to tell the guys at the water department that there's a main busted somewhere and they need to come fix it. I'm going to want a nice hot shower in about three or four hours."

Still thirsty, you make your way to the kitchen and open up the refrigerator to see how much orange juice is left. Even though the refrigerator light isn't working, you can tell the pitcher is empty. Fortunately, there's one more can of OJ in the freezer, which seems to be thawing out. But, oh yeah, the water isn't working, so you can't make more juice anyway.

Guess what? The situation isn't about to improve anytime soon. You've been awake for all of five minutes and now you're getting a taste of just how much we all depend on water. In fact, we can't live long without it, let alone get a quick cure for cottonmouth or enjoy a nice shower once you fully awaken.

The bad news is that the guys over at the water department aren't going to be coming out to your neighborhood because there's no break in the water lines to be fixed. The problem is much greater than that. Many water treatment plants around the country have shutdown as a result of computers shutting down—the computers that turned from 12/31/99 to 1/1/00 overnight. The computers have crashed, caused the water treatment systems to malfunction, or the systems have lost electrical power. Lack of power has also idled the pumping equipment and/or the computers that regulate the pumps. After a few seconds of jettisoning whatever water you have left in the pipes to your home, they are running dry. You are now officially without water, and you have no idea when it's going to come back on, or even if it's going to be potable once the water supply is restored—in two days, two weeks, two months—who knows?

What Happened to the Water?

People are often dumbfounded when the subject of water comes up during discussions about Y2K preparedness. How could Y2K affect our water? Most of us take the availability of water for granted making it hard to believe that water could be an issue. Trust us, it is an issue—a serious one.

Most of us living in cities, towns, and even rural areas get our water from large dams, rivers, and reservoirs. Piped in, often from long distances (unless you're on your own well), this water is channeled through water treatment plants that filter and chemically treat water to assure its drinkability. Unfortunately, many treatment plants and water delivery systems are managed and regulated by computers and embedded microchips, some of which could malfunction on Jan. 1, 2000.

Water treatment plants depend on computers and chips to control things like water flow, the amount of chemicals released into the water supply each day, and water testing systems. They also rely on the delivery of chemicals to treat the water and payment for those chemicals through banking transactions, which is all dependent on computers. If these systems fail, it could contaminate our drinking water, endangering our communities. So even if there *is* water coming out of your faucets, it might not be suitable for drinking. The water coming through your pipes on January 1, 2000, might look clear and therefore clean, but maybe it isn't.

Officials at one treatment plant said they could handle any problem, if necessary, with their backup generator. When asked how much fuel they had stored for the generator, they said three days' worth—enough for a typical power outage after a hurricane or tornado. Sorry, that won't cut it. Their faces went blank when pressed further about power outages that might last longer than three days.

Even if all the steps in the process work and the water gets treated, there is another system that regulates the *delivery* of our water. Most treatment plants depend on electricity to pump the water and the billing system to record payments so your water is not turned off inadvertently. It is our feeling (or hope) that if billing systems were the only operation breakdown to occur that overrides would be implemented to provide water to everyone, regardless of payment status, until the problem was fixed.

These are some of the major reasons why you should store some water long before January 1, 2000, and then be prepared to treat your water supply after your stored water is gone. If you've stored two weeks of clean water, and the Y2K crisis drags on longer, then you've got a problem unless you can find another source of water and treat it to make it drinkable.

The rest of this chapter explains procedures for:

> **A. Water Storage**
> **B. Water Treatment**
> **C. Water Sources**

A. Water Storage

Experts say we can go a week or more without food before suffering serious health complications. Most people, however, can only go three or four days without water. Even if the Y2K crisis lasts *only* five to seven days, you will be in serious trouble without potable (drinkable) water at hand. Knowing how to store potable water should be one of your top priorities when preparing for any disaster, and the Y2K crisis is no exception.

Luckily, proper water storage is not difficult. It's up to you to decide for how long a period of time you need to prepare. But if you're preparing to have, for example, a month's supply of food stored up for Y2K, then it would make sense for you to store or be able to treat up to a month's worth of drinking water and a month's worth of water for other uses such as cooking, bathing, and flushing the toilet.

The average person needs to drink two quarts of water a day but requirements can vary depending upon age, physical activity, and diet. Here are some special considerations to keep in mind as guidelines:

- People who live in hot climates require more water due to perspiration and evaporation from the skin.
- In addition to drinking water, more is needed for food preparation and hygiene. Water for these purposes needs to be drinkable since harmful microorganisms and other contaminants can be passed on from cooking or brushing your teeth.
- Plan on storing more water for children, mothers who are nursing infants, and people who are ill. With these special needs, additional supply is required due to increased demand for cleanliness. Things like sterilizing bottles, washing clothes, and general hygiene all require more water.

1. Quantity(ies) of Stored Water   Okay, let's talk a little more about storing water. It's very simple. The rule of thumb is to store a minimum of two weeks' worth of water, one gallon per day per person. One half gallon is for drinking, the other half is for cooking, bathing, and washing dishes. Unfortunately, things like long, hot baths and washing machines go "down the drain," so to speak, in an emergency. This is survival here.

At over eight pounds per gallon, water is heavy to store and takes up a lot of space. For this reason, beyond storing for a couple of days (at the most, a couple of weeks), ongoing water needs should be handled with water treatment, which is discussed in more detail later. Also, be wary of water coming into your home after Y2K for it may still need to be purified for drinking. If you don't have running water, the stored water will tide you over while you find, collect, and treat water from another source, like from a creek, rainwater, or snowmelt.

Let's take our calculations out to a water preparedness chart that accounts for different numbers of people occupying your home and also allow for various lengths of Y2K crisis "down time." The figures are based on one gallon of water per person for each day of the Y2K crisis. For the purpose of this sample, let's look at how much *drinking* and *other* water you would need to store for one week, three weeks, and six weeks.

Potable Water Storage

	One week	Three weeks	Six weeks
Number of family Members			
Number of gallons per member	X 1	X 1	X1
Subtotal	=	=	=
Multiply for total supply	X 7	X 21	X 42
Total minimum gallons for family	=	=	=

Non-potable Water Storage

	One week	Three weeks	Six weeks
Number of family members			
Number of gallons per member	X 2	X 2	X 2
Subtotal	=	=	=
Multiply for total supply	X 7	X 21	X 42
Total minimum gallons for family	=	=	=

2. Method(s) of Storing Water Store water in clean plastic or glass containers with tight screw-on lids. Water lasts indefinitely if properly stored. There are a few other important considerations to help you select containers for water storage:

- Heavy-duty five gallon plastic water containers are convenient and safe to use. These are inexpensive and readily available at major discount stores like Target, Kmart, and

Wal-Mart. They hold a good amount of water, but are portable so that you can carry full containers into the kitchen or bathroom as needed.

- Glass containers with metal lids, like used juice bottles, are good since glass doesn't release any chemicals into the water or absorb odors like plastic can over time. However, since they are breakable so they must be stored and handled with care.

- Plastic water bottles or empty soft drink bottles are fine (and cheap!) but some experts say they should be emptied and used within six months since they can crack over time. Also, chemical agents in the bottles can leach into the water eventually.

- Never use a container that has held toxic substances like garden chemicals, gasoline or automobile oil.

- Avoid containers like milk cartons that can fall apart easily.

- For larger supplies of water, you can also get food-grade plastic buckets or drums that come in fifteen gallon ($30), thirty gallon ($45), and fifty-five gallon ($60) sizes from emergency preparedness outlets and catalogs. (*See Major Surplus and Supply in Preparedness Resources on page 184.*)

Water Preparedness Tip on New Year's Eve:
Forget the Bubbly and Think Water!

Fill all bathtubs, sinks, and spare garbage cans (clean) with water to use for flushing toilets and other non-drinkable uses.

Water Preparedness Chart

The chart below presents the minimum amount of water you need to plan for, depending on the number of people in your household.*

Family members	3 days	1 week	2 weeks	1 month	3 months
1 Person	3 gal	7 gal	14 gal	30 gal	90 gal
2 People	6 gal	14 gal	28 gal	60 gal	180 gal
3 People	9 gal	21 gal	42 gal	90 gal	270 gal
4 People	12 gal	28 gal	56 gal	120 gal	360 gal
5 People	15 gal	35 gal	70 gal	150 gal	450 gal
6 People	18 gal	42 gal	84 gal	180 gal	540 gal

For the light shaded areas, focus on storing water in plastic juice and soft drink containers or glass jars with tight-fitting lids.	For the medium shaded areas, focus on storing water in larger containers like 15, 30, and 55 gallon food-grade plastic buckets or drums.	For the heavy shaded areas, focus on a good water treatment plan rather than storing.

*In addition to the potable water that you store and/or treat, fill garbage cans, bathtubs and other large vessels with nondrinking water that you may need to flush toilets, in case water isn't running at all.

NOTE - The chart shows storage strategies for up to one month of *stored* water. Then, it shows amounts of water to *collect and treat* following the first two weeks of using stored water. If you have the storage room and capacity to store and/or treat more, increase amounts to suit your needs. **No matter how much water you plan to store, you should have a good water treatment plan.**

B. Water Treatment

Long-term emergency water needs, beyond your initial stored water supply, should be handled by treating water. Treating water is simply the process of purifying it to make it safe to drink.

Don't assume that if you have running water following December 31, 1999, that the water is drinkable. Contact local water treatment officials to determine whether the water is safe and use stored water until you are confident that it is indeed drinkable. Fortunately, treating water is easy to do.

Under normal conditions, water treatment plants treat our drinking water for us by running it through a series of filters and injecting chemical additives like chlorine to kill microorganisms, remove toxic chemicals, and debris so that it's safe to use by the time it comes through our faucets at home. Some water treatment plants could suffer problems from either malfunctioning computer programs or microchips that implement faulty treatment processes or stop altogether and thus, put the safety of our water in question. Also, if the power were to go out, it could prevent water delivery completely, since pumps that deliver water to your home rely on electricity.

Handling your own water treatment may sound complicated but it's really very easy with proper preparations. In fact, treatment should be a priority to minimize the amount of water you have to store. If you try to store enough water to survive a month or two, you'll find yourself overrun with water bottles, or have an overload of giant drums that weigh a ton and take up half your garage.

The two-week supply of water that you store should allow plenty of time to collect water from other sources, if necessary. As you use water, replenish your supply. Don't wait until you're almost out of stored water before you begin to locate and collect water from outside sources. Snow or rain water is a readily available source. A swimming pool or hot tub can function as a private reservoir, since the chlorine in your pool is no different than the chlorine water treatment plants use to treat city water. However, it is advisable to run this water through a water purifier or boil it before use. Also, streams or lakes are additional sources of water. Be sure to have containers to transport it.

A Special Note: Water failure beyond two weeks is a worst-case scenario given that restoring service will be such a high priority. However, even if water is coming into your home, it is not necessarily properly treated. Also, if you are in a small community or rural area, the risks for prolonged water problems are greater where some power failures affecting water delivery could last longer than in urban areas. Rural areas will be the lowest priority to restore power.

Should availability of water or water impurity remain a problem beyond a couple of weeks, it could create a serious public health crisis. Problems stemming from poor sanitation and illness could be overwhelming for health care and emergency services. For this reason, it is crucial that you practice cleanliness, health, and safety in all that you do. (For more information review chapters on "Health, Hygiene, and Medical Issues" and "Sanitation and Refuse.")

There will most likely be only remote and isolated incidents of water delivery failures, however, for the full safety of your family, it is best to be prepared to treat water beyond what has been stored.

Remember, just because water looks clear does not mean it is safe to drink. In other words, it's what you can't see that can be especially dangerous to your health. In an emergency, always assume an alternative water supply is contaminated and perhaps even your main supply. That's the bad news. The good news is that water is not hard to safely treat.

1. Why Treat Your Water   To understand emergency water treatment, it's useful to know a little about water problems so that you can better decide on how you want to treat your water. Untreated water can contain many contaminants including microorganisms: pathogenic cysts (Giardia and Cryptosporidia), bacteria (Typhoid and Cholera), and viruses (Hepatitis A & B); and chemicals: lead (from plumbing), Lindane & Atrazine (from pesticides), and chlorine (from water treatment plants). The largest and easiest to strain (with filters, purifiers, chemicals, or boiling) microorganisms are the pathogenic cysts. Bacteria are smaller and more difficult to remove (with purifiers, chemicals, or boiling) while viruses are tiniest and must be removed by using a high quality water purifier, chemicals, or boiling.

Water Contaminant Chart

This chart reviews some of the common contaminants that you want to guard against as best you can. High-quality water purifiers and water filters (used with chlorine) will eliminate all or most of them.

Microorganism	Source	Effect
Cryptosporidium & Giardia	• Primary source is animal feces which can contain harmful cysts. • Land run-off carries cysts into lakes, streams and rivers where water treatment plants collect the water. • The cyst microorganism is small (3-4 microns in size) with a hard shell that protects	• The EPA estimates that 155 million people are potentially at risk from waterborne cryptosporidium. • Can cause flu-like symptoms that can last one to three weeks in healthy adults. • Can be life-threatening for persons with suppressed immune systems,

Water Contamination Chart (*continued*)

Microorganism	Source	Effect
	it from chlorine, the most commonly used disinfectant in municipal waste treatment plants.	such as HIV/AIDS and cancer patients.
Lead	• Lead can leach into water from lead plumbing, lead solder and brass alloy faucets.	• Chronic hazard that can cause lower IQs, memory reduction, and shorter attention spans in children. • Can cause damage to red blood cells and kidneys, and promote high blood pressure in adults.
Lindane & Atrazine	• Lindane is a pesticide used on cattle, lumber, and gardens. • Atrazine is a herbicide used on corn and non-crop land. • Chemicals may move down through the soil into groundwater or carried into lakes and rivers by rain water runoff.	• Lindane can cause liver, immune, circulatory, and nerve problems. • Atrazine can cause mammary gland tumors.
Mercury	• Direct and indirect water contamination can result from crop runoff, natural deposits, batteries, and electrical switches.	• Kidney and nervous system disorders.
Chlorine	• Disinfectants used by drinking water treatment plants.	• Chlorine-treated water can be responsible for bad taste and odor.

("Is Your Drinking Water Safe?" U.S. Environmental Protection Agency, May 1994)

2. How To Treat Your Water   Here's a quick look at the three most common approaches for water treatment. **Water Filters and Purifiers** are reliable, and a certified water purifier is probably the best method for all-around, convenient protection to eliminate most, if not all, contaminants, depending on the quality of the unit. Water filters are not as powerful as water purifiers but are certainly effective against many contaminants. **Chemical Treatment** is effective against viruses and bacteria, but ineffective against some cysts. It also causes the water to have a strong chemical odor and taste. **Boiling** protects against all three forms of microbiological contaminants, including cysts, bacteria, and viruses. However, boiling does nothing to remove chemicals and actually increases concentrations because as you boil water some of it evaporates as steam.

Now, let's take a detailed look at each of these methods so you can decide what's best for you:

a. Water Filters and Purifiers   Quality water purifiers are used all over the world by travelers, international aid workers, and emergency relief organizations like the Red Cross and many more, to ensure pure drinking water. Water purifiers are a tried and true method of treating water.

A quality hand pump or gravity feed water purifier is the optimum choice for any emergency preparedness kit. These kinds of purifiers offer the best water treatment security in an emergency since they remove most, if not all, harmful contaminants and are able to operate without electricity or water pressure. It's important to review the pros and cons of whatever purifier or filter you buy with your local dealer or Y2K preparedness supplier. (*See Clean Water Chart on page 56.*) Be careful when buying filters because some remove only tastes and odors, whereas others remove cysts, but only water purifiers will remove cysts as well as bacteria and viruses. (Under federal guidelines, only those products certified to the EPA Microbiological Standards to protect against all three types of disease organisms can legally be described as drinking water purifiers.)

Among the portable units, water *purifiers* tend to be more expensive than water *filters* since filters do not have all the contaminant removing capabilities so purifiers are the best choice. A decent water filter will remove parasitic cysts (such as Cryptosporidia and Giardia) but may not protect against viruses or even bacteria. If you use a water filter to eliminate cysts, just add some bleach to the water to take care of the viruses and bacteria. (Talk to your local camping dealer, Jade Mountain 800-442-1972, or General Ecology 610-363-7900 about what would work best for you.)

Since the Y2K crisis could cause problems with water pressure, you want a portable water purifier that you can operate even in areas without dependable water pressure. This is why a hand pump or gravity feed unit is a better all-around choice rather than the typical residential models often thought of when talking about water purification systems since water has to come through the faucet for these to function. After all, you may not be able to purify your water from a household water tap but rather from one container to another. If this sounds a lot like camping, it is.

Now let's review the advantages and disadvantages of filters and purifiers:

Advantages:

- Filters are affordable, portable, and require no fuel.
- Purifiers can be affordable, can be portable, and can be hand pumped; they also filter out all cysts, bacteria, and viruses. The best purifiers are EPA certified.

Disadvantages:

- Filters do not remove viruses and can be negligible in their filtration.

- Filters do not have to be certified by the EPA. Purifiers can be expensive and the noncarbon filtration systems do not remove chemicals or bad tastes.

The following is a description of some of the best and most common water purifiers available:

Katadyn Filters   These filters are manufactured in Switzerland and are nicely made. Katadyn has been on the market with their silver impregnated, ceramic candle filters for many years. Ceramic filters are designed to remove the organic materials like cysts and bacteria, but not chemicals. Katadyn offers a "Combi" unit which also includes a charcoal filter that will remove the chemicals like chlorine. Katadyn also offers a gravity feed drip filter that is good for high volume. To use the gravity feed filters, simply pour the water into the top of the unit and it will feed water slowly through the device and come out clean and ready to dispense through the bottom spout. The hand pump units are faster.

Advantages:

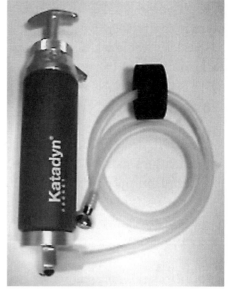

- They are smooth, reliable, and easy to operate.
- Katadyn performed very well as a filter against bacteria and cysts during an industry-wide test series in 1995.

Disadvantages:

- Ceramic elements are so fine and dense

Katadyn water filter

Courtesy of Jade Mountain

it clogs quickly with sediment and requires extra force of
pumping action to use.

- Care must be used to prevent contamination during the filter cleaning process by cleaning it with filtered water.
- It is not certified for virus protection, which can be elimi-
nated with chlorine or iodine tablets. Fortunately, viral
contamination is not a big problem in the United States.
- Prices range from $100 to $300. (Available from Jade
Mountain.)

General Ecology Purifiers General Ecology's "Structured Matrix" is certified to remove all three types of disease microorganisms without the use of chemicals, electricity, double pumping, or
added holding time. It meets the EPA's microbiological purifier
standards. It also removes many chemical contaminants and foul
tastes and odors as well. (The General Ecology Company purifiers
treat much of the water you drink on commercial airline flights.)

General Ecology offers both portable and residential units.
The portable units include a fast flowing system that has a kit to
test the filtration canisters (First Need Deluxe). The other
portable system is good for groups because it has a two quart per
minute flow rate (Base Camp). This model has been used in many
of the most treacherous climbing exhibitions to Mount Everest
and other mountain peaks. General Ecology also offers residential
units that are installed to a kitchen tap. These units require water
delivery, which relies on electricity. You can purchase an adapter
kit ($140) that converts the purifier to a portable pump.

Advantages:

- Their outstanding quality, filterability, and ease of use.
- They are reasonably priced, considering their structured
matrix micro-strainer filtration system.

General Ecology water purifiers

Disadvantage:

- They are not as readily available as Katadyn and PŪR systems. (Call Essentials 2000 at 800-775-1991 or General
  Ecology at 610-363-7900 to find a dealer closest to you.)

PŪR The PŪR Company (pronounced "pure") offers several readily available filters and iodine-based purifiers for both domestic and portable use. You can find them at most camping and sporting goods stores. PŪR has advertised "no clogging" as an advantage, but you should know that clogging can serve a purpose of telling you the filter is no longer doing its job. As the purifier is used, it reduces the chemical agents in the unit that eliminate the harmful microorganisms. So, make sure you change filters regularly.

The hiking and travel industries have relied on PŪR's small portable water filters and purifiers for healthy travel around the world. They're small, lightweight (often less than 1 pound), and reasonable in cost. The filters range from $35 to $60, and the purifiers range from $90 to $130. The best purifiers strain water through a filter composed of a complex matrix of micro-pores, generally with iodine filters, which allows the water to flow through but destroys bacteria and viruses. It is important to recognize that chemical treatment effectiveness is dependent on having both adequate amounts of the chemical pesticide and enough contact time for both the iodine, chlorine, or other chemicals to work. Tests have shown that double pumping and adding holding time can increase the effectiveness of these units.

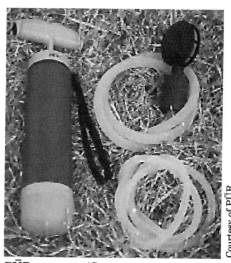

Courtesy of PŪR

PŪR water purifier

Advantages:

- Their "no clogging" features.
- The filters are inexpensive and work well to eliminate bacteria and cysts.
- The purifiers are also quite affordable and offer protection against bacteria, cysts, and viruses.
- Their availability; PŪR is one of the most common brands sold at camping stores.

Disadvantages:

- They do not protect against viruses, which aren't a big problem in the United States unless the sewage gets backed up.
- Because it's hard to tell when the filter is spent, you will have to change them more often.

Clean Water Chart

	Removes[1]	Filter Medium	Price/ Replacement filter element[2]	Output (ltr/min)
FILTERS				
Katadyn				
Pocket	C,G,B	Ceramic micro-strainer	$249 / $165	0.50
TRX Drip	C,G,B	Ceramic micro-strainer	$275 / NA	0.03
PŪR				
Pioneer	C,G,B	Glassfiber disk	$35 / $8 (for 2)	1.02
Hiker	C,G,B	Pleated glassfiber	$60 / $30	1.50
PURIFIERS				
General Ecology				
First Need Deluxe	C,G,B,V	Structured matrix micro-strainer	$75 / $33	1.34

Clean Water Chart (*continued*)

Base Camp	C,G,B,V	Structured matrix micro-strainer	$466 / $62	2.11
NaturePure Ultrafine	C,G,B,V		NA	
Seagull IV-X	C,G,B,V		NA	
PŪR				
Scout	C,G,B,V	Iodine resin/ glassfiber/carbon	$90 / $45	1.57
Voyageur	C,G,B,V	Iodine resin/ pleated glassfiber/ carbon	$75 / $40	1.30
Explorer	C,G,B,V	Tri-iodine resin/ glassfiber	$130 / $50	1.20

[1]C=Cryposporidia, G=Giardia, B=Bacteria, V=Viruses

[2]The first amount is for the actual filter or purifier. The second amount is for the replacement filter element—the cartridge that actually does the filtering. These cartridges vary in the amount of water they can treat. These prices are subject to change as demand increases.

All filters wear out eventually with use so take the precaution of buying extra filters for whatever system you choose and read the manufacturers' instructions on how often to change them. No one knows how long Y2K problems could last, so you may also want to invest in some parts in case you need to do minor repairs on your purifier.

b. Chemical Treatment Water is commonly treated with a chemical such as chlorine bleach. Use any unscented household liquid bleach that contains 5.25 percent sodium hypochlorite and no soap. (You probably already have some in your laundry room.) Add four drops of bleach or iodine per quart of water with an eyedropper (or two scant teaspoons per ten gallons), and stir. Seal your containers tightly, label them clearly, and store them in a cool, dark place. Let us warn you, this type of water treatment calls for moderate levels of chlorine, which means the water won't taste like a swimming pool but will have a scent and taste of chlorine.

Chlorine, when used correctly, disinfectants against bacteria and viruses but does not protect against Cryptosporidia and Giardia. With this type of treatment you are at risk of exposure to these cysts. Iodine water treatment tablets, which you can buy from your local camping supply store, will get rid of Giardia but not Cryptosporidia. Follow manufacturers' instructions on the bottle. Chlorine and iodine are not fail-safe, but they do offer decent protection.

Now let's review the advantages and disadvantages to chemical treatment:

Advantages:

- Chemical treatment is easy to do and requires no mechanisms that may break or clog.
- Chlorine bleach kills bacteria and viruses.
- Iodine kills bacteria, viruses, and Giardia.

Disadvantages:

- These chemicals make the water taste funny.
- Neither chlorine nor iodine protect against Cryptosporidia.

c. Boiling Boiling water at a rolling boil for ten minutes in a big pot on your stove, which may be a camping stove, protects against all three types of disease microorganisms. However, there are several disadvantages to boiling. Boiling water takes lots of time and energy to heat and then cool so it's refreshing to drink. While this may be okay for a day or two, if the electric and gas utilities in your area shut down, boiling water may not be practical as you will need to conserve as much fuel as possible. Also, boiling doesn't remove nonvolatile chemical contaminants and actually increases the concentration of these contaminants because some water escapes as steam. Another disadvantage is that boiled water has a funny taste because it lacks oxygen. If you do rely on boiling your water, it tastes better if you aerate it by pouring it back and forth between two clean containers. Washed out, used soda bottles are fine to use for this. (Aerate your stored water, too, for better taste.)

For adequate Y2K water treatment preparation, you need to take precautions that assume you may not be able to boil water. The best preparations are to be able to treat your water by a variety of methods.

Now let's review the advantages and disadvantages to boiling:

Advantages:

- Boiling kills all three types of microorganisms.
- It requires the least amount of preparation.

Disadvantages:

- Boiling requires a lot of energy, doesn't remove chemicals, and actually increases their concentration.
- It also makes the water taste funny.

C. Water Sources

In the unlikely event that the Y2K crisis causes a lengthy shutdown of water delivery—either by computer regulating systems shutting down or power failures that don't allow water pumping systems to function—then you'll have to look around to replenish the water that you've stored.

Here are some suggestions for additional emergency water supplies:

1. Additional Water Sources The following are some additional water sources if water delivery is out longer than your stored water lasts:

▸ **Water heater** Drain the water out of the tank by turning off the water supply line coming into the tank and open the faucet located at the bottom of the tank to drain into a water container. Make sure that the gas or electricity is turned off.

▸ **Hot tub or swimming pool**   If you have one, it can become a private reservoir. Chlorine may not make it taste too good, but it's the same chlorine used by treatment plants. Run the water through a water purifier if you have one.

▸ **Ice cubes**   Use the water in the ice cube trays in the freezer.

▸ **Bathtubs and sinks**   Fill bathtubs and sinks with water on December 31, 1999, in case water supplies are disrupted. This supply could be useful for flushing toilets.

▸ **Pipes**   Drain the water out of your home's pipes. Turn off the main water line coming into your house—this could also prevent sewage backup. Locate the main line ahead of time as they sometimes require a special tool that can be purchased at the hardware store. Turn on the faucet in the highest location in the house to allow air in the pipes. Then, turn on all the faucets going down to the one in the lowest location. Use a bucket to collect water from outdoor spigots, particularly the one that is lowest on the gravity chain so that as much water in the house's pipes will flow to the lowest faucet.

2. Emergency Water Sources The following are emergency water sources in the unlikely event that water delivery will be out for extended periods of time:

▸ **Rainwater** Simply place a clean bucket under your drain spout so that rather then letting it pour into a planting bed or all over the sidewalk, you're adding to your water supply.

▸ **Snow** Many of you will be surrounded by plenty of snow. Start collecting it into clean buckets or bins and bring it indoors by a heat source so that it can melt slowly on its own. If the power were to go out, you don't want to waste precious fuel to melt snow if you don't have to.

▸ **Streams, rivers, ponds, and lakes** If you have to resort to this method of collecting, you may have to carry water some distance. Use manageable containers, like one gallon water jugs or soda bottles that are easy to carry. Lighten your load with a wheel barrow or a child's wagon and you'll be able to carry more. Get the children involved in helping with this.

••Best Recommendation for Water Treatment••

Be prepared to use all three methods of treating water. The best purifier is a hand-pump or gravity feed water filter or purifier for your Y2K preparedness lifeboat. No electricity or water pressure is required to use. Have two extra filters and replacement parts on hand.

CHAPTER 3

POWER

"I think we're no longer at the point of asking whether or not there will be any power disruptions, but we are now forced to ask how severe the disruptions are going to be. If we don't have power to generate electricity, everything else is moot."

—Senator Dodd (D-Connecticut)

"When you consider how important our electric utilities are to everything we do in life, then you'll realize that if we do not have our compliance for Y2K and as things fall apart, it's going to be devastating in our entire society."

—Representative Connie Morella (R-Maryland)

Our dependence on electricity is staggering. It is best to get a grip on the implications of Y2K national power outages now so you can prepare. Brief power outages are common during an electrical storm or after a construction worker has cut through the power line in your neighborhood. These power outages usually last thirty minutes to an hour and are more of an annoyance than a disruption of lifestyle. Those of us who have been in ice or wind storms and had to tough it out for several hours or even days without electricity can testify to the real hardships of life without power over a longer period of time.

If you think being without food or water for a week or more would be bad, think about how much worse it would get without power, too. How much of a hardship is this going to cause? Living without power for a week or more can be a major hardship if caught unprepared. Even if you're not a glutton for punishment, you might want to consider giving yourself a dry run to test your mental readiness for the coming crisis, or at least remind yourself of what the loss of electricity would do to your lifestyle. Wait until about sunset some early evening, then shut off all your circuit breakers, except the refrigerator if you've just spent $200 on groceries. Then try going at least twelve to twenty-four hours without electricity to see what it feels like.

Here's what happens: all the electrical clocks stop; the TVs, CD players, stereos, and radios don't work; the air conditioning or the heat, depending on what time of year it is, shuts down; none of the lights will work; all of the appliances are as dead as a doornail; and even the electrically powered garage door won't budge. And that's just in the first two minutes. Over time, the refrigerator (if you went ahead and turned off its breaker, too) and freezer start to thaw out; the water coming out of your faucet or shower gradually gets lukewarm and then room temperature; your laptop computer goes blank after about ninety minutes of battery operation; and the temperature inside your house becomes very cold or sweltering, depending on the season. Everything becomes very still in your house, where in your experiment you still have the security of knowing you can power back up at any time. Besides, the lights are still on all over the rest of your neighborhood.

So, what's happening here? How could a Y2K computer glitch cause a power shutdown? An interruption in food supplies is understandable because stores and distribution centers rely on computers and computerized just-in-time shipping. But this is different, isn't it? After all, electricity is electricity, and as long as the power lines are up and the circuits are open, what's to stop me from heating up a frozen dinner in the microwave oven?

The delivery of electricity should be smooth, the status quo of modern life, right? Unfortunately for all of us, the electric industry is vulnerable to Y2K breakdowns on several fronts and thus, could cause our electric service to go down as quickly as flipping off a light switch. Computers and embedded chips from within the power plant or utility company itself regulate and manage both electricity *production* and power *distribution* to you, the customer. The problem is that many of these systems are difficult to test, particularly the embedded chips because they are so hard to find and isolate. There are also secondary Y2K issues. To generate electricity, some power companies rely on timely shipments of coal, oil, or natural gas for their own operation. If there are Y2K-related breakdowns in the railway system and trucking industries, which again rely heavily on computers, then these deliveries don't get made, and the power companies cannot generate power.

In some ways, the biggest risk stems from the vast complexity of the system itself because there are so many computers and embedded chips that, combined with another often overlooked ingredient, human error, will likely cause at least some regional and local system breakdowns.

Some Y2K experts believe that if the power grid goes down in various regions, Herculean efforts would be made to restore power to at least the large urban areas within two weeks. There's little doubt that the more-populated areas will be the top priority, so if you live in a more remote area, you should be prepared to handle your own needs for at least a month.

No Power to the Power Grid

The power grid is composed of a huge sprawling and interconnected system of nearly four thousand power companies, including 108 nuclear power plants. To visualize the overlapping connectedness of the power grid, think of the whole system as a giant pyramid divided into thirds. At the top of the pyramid are four major "interconnect" regions that make up the entire grid for the United

States and parts of Canada and Mexico. These four regions are: 1) the Eastern Interconnect (from the Atlantic to the Continental Divide), 2) the Western Interconnect (from the Continental Divide to the Pacific), 3) the Texas Interconnect called IRCOT (three-quarters of Texas), and 4) the Quebec Interconnect (part of East Coast and Canada). Each of these four regions are then broken into eleven regional operating councils, which can be viewed as the middle part of the pyramid. At the bottom of the pyramid are about two hundred "control areas." Although there are around four thousand electric companies that provide power to these control areas, 75 percent of all the electricity generated in the United States comes from only three hundred electric companies. The interconnectedness of this system allows electricity to be exchanged, controlled, and distributed between regions and control areas where needed. Rick Cowles, utility expert and author of *Electric Utilities and Y2K* says that "a Y2K problem at any level has the potential to propagate through the entire pyramid."

Edward Yourdon, author of *Timebomb 2000* and twenty-five other books on software and computers, said in 1998, "the '00' might make [computers] think ... it's been ninety-eight years since they were last calibrated and tell them to shut the plant down. If that happens to be a utility plant, that means the lights go out." Only one of the three staple industries—utilities, telecommunications, or banking—needs to go down to cause massive social chaos, because these industries are all integrally linked and together form the cornerstones of our civilized world.

Now, let's look at nuclear power plants in particular, since so many people have expressed fears that radiation could be released inadvertently as a result of computer failures. Nuclear power plants are an important source of energy, generating about 20 percent of the nation's electricity overall. The good news is that the nuclear power industry is tightly regulated by the Nuclear Regulatory Commission (NRC). They have the authority to shut down any nuclear plant—on demand—and they will, even if there is only the slightest doubt that it is not compliant. No one knows what the final outcome will be, and won't until as late as December, as to whether any plants will be shut down. It takes only about twelve hours to safely shut down a plant. It appears that the greatest danger is not from some horrible nuclear exposure but more from compromised power production stemming from plant shutdowns. This would be especially troublesome for the East Coast where this large and populated area depends on 40 to 60 percent of its energy from nuclear power.

Anyone talking about the grid going down risks sounding like an extremist, yet many knowledgeable experts, and even U.S. senators, see a real possibility of at least regional blackouts.

"I think we're no longer at the point of asking whether or not there will be any power disruptions, but we are now forced to ask how severe the disruptions are going to be. If we don't have power to generate electricity, everything else is moot," warns Senator Dodd. To add to the mystery, no one can pinpoint where those failures are likely to be.

"I think we face the prospect of some degree of chaos—blackouts, brownouts, possibly some degree of phone outages, possibly some bank failures . . . Some people are optimistic and think they'll manage to fix all the computer systems; others, like me, who have worked in the computer business and have seen how all of these things can get messed up—some of us are considerably more pessimistic," cautions Ed Yourdon.

The utility industry was late to recognize the Y2K threat, but over the last year and a half they have jumped on it like a fireman racing to save his own house. Experts believe that there are enough protections now in place that the prospect of the entire grid shutting down is remote. However, it is likely that there will be some regional blackouts lasting anywhere from a few days to weeks, or longer. There could also be cascading failures within the grid where many minor problems add to up to bigger ones over the first days and weeks in January. This domino effect could cause power problems to worsen into the middle of January. So January 1, 2000, might not be the worst day for power outages.

More common power problems are likely to stem from *limited* power production because of nuclear power plant shutdowns and other power plants not being able to function due to computer failures and/or lack of fuel (coal, oil, natural gas) to operate. Blackouts or brownouts could easily result. There could be a lot less electricity to go around, which would force the utility companies to ration power. The top priority in allocating power is for emergency services such as hospitals and police. The next people to get power would probably be residential customers who live in cities followed by residents in rural areas. The third priority in power allocation would probably be commercial business and industry. Using the analogy of electricity being like water, instead of being able to take showers whenever we want, wash the car, water the yard, we may have to "drink" only what electricity we absolutely need.

When talking about Y2K power problems, the word "brownout" is mentioned frequently. What is a brownout? Brownouts, also called "dirty power," are spikes and surges of power that are caused by uneven delivery, like when lightning strikes and the lights flicker. Y2K could cause minor power plant disruptions that last only a few minutes or more, then "spike" when the power resumes again. This can result in the damaging of electronic appliances and especially sensitive electronic equipment like computers and sound systems. To prevent damage, keep your sensitive electronic equipment unplugged whenever you aren't using it for at least several weeks after January. Spikes can even damage equipment that is not turned on. Don't think your surge protector will always protect everything. All it takes is one strong spike to destroy a lot of surge protectors. Unfortunately, it is difficult to know if you are getting hit with bad spikes. If lights are flickering, however, that is an immediate indication to unplug your stuff, including your surge protector (might as well protect it, too). I learned the hard way by blowing out two computer motherboards when living in an old apartment building that had a lot of spikes. Your best insurance is to change surge protectors often.

Brownout Tips

Don't forget to protect your sensitive electronic equipment like computers and sound systems. Unplug them when not in use and buy extra surge protectors to replace the used ones.

How to Prepare for a Power Failure

Nothing will return us to nineteenth-century living faster than a collapse of the power grid. Though a total collapse is unlikely, the possibility of localized blackouts remains strong. Of course, it would be a lot easier on all of us if we knew *where* these blackouts might hit so we could focus Y2K preparation efforts just on those areas but alas, we don't. That's why we have to assume it could affect all areas and make adequate preparations.

Being prepared for a breakdown of the power grid during the Y2K crisis requires more knowledge of technical matters than does knowing how to deal with shortages of food and water. There is no *one* correct way to work through the long-term loss of electricity at your home. There are options and solutions to deal with the basic needs of heating, cooking, and lighting that are right for you. If you decide, for example, that buying a generator isn't practical or doesn't fit into your Y2K budget, then skip that section and move on. This chapter is broken down into three main parts, each of which explains the situation and suggests what you need to do:

> **A. Energy Conservation**
> **B. Alternative Power Supplies**
> **C. Heating, Cooking, and Lighting**

A. Energy Conservation

Regardless of how you plan to heat your home or provide light during a power outage, it is essential to maximize your home's energy efficiency. A good analogy is your financial balance sheet: The quickest way to increase your spendable income is to decrease your expenses. This idea of energy efficiency, or energy savings, applies to anyone, whether you live in a house or apartment. If you're in a situation where every bit of wood and fuel counts, it's crucial that basic energy conservation measures are taken before January 2000.

More than 50 percent of our annual energy bills go toward space heating alone, and this percentage increases in colder climates. This is why basic energy conservation goes a long way in retaining heat (and cool, for that matter, if you live in a hot climate). Can you believe the average American house has enough air leaks to make up what would amount to a four-foot-square hole in the side of your home? It's true!

Weatherizing your home can be inexpensive, and you don't have to be an expert. Any home center or hardware store carries all the energy conservation supplies you need: door threshold, weather stripping, caulk, and fluorescent bulbs. First, close off any parts of the house you're not using. Don't forget to shut off the heating vents, too. Even if you don't have major blackouts, there still could be intermittent power failures for short periods, so there's no point in wasting whatever heat you can get. Taking steps to conserve the energy in your home will help retain (or repel) the heat during a loss of electricity. Your investment will begin to pay off immediately by reducing the size of your energy bills.

By dealing with energy conservation first, you can help yourself in a Y2K power outage by reducing the amount of energy you may need in your home for heat. Let's take a closer look at how to increase the energy efficiency in your home by studying the following three areas:

1. Doors and Windows
2. Insulation
3. Lighting

1. Doors and Windows   Install a good quality threshold with a rubber gasket to close the gaps under your outside doors. They come in standard sizes, but if you need to make adjustments, they're easy to trim with a saw. Then just screw them into place.

Next, apply weather stripping around the rest of the door and your windows, too. I like the kind of weather stripping that provides little brads to tack it into place, but you can also get stuff that just tapes into place. If it's sealed tightly, you should have to tug on the door to close it. Check all the doors and windows in your house or apartment. Seal the outside door and window trim (the frame around the door or window) with durable silicone caulk.

Weatherizing products are available at any home center or hardware store. Costs of products vary depending on the quality you buy, but they are all reasonable.

2. Insulation   This is a bigger job than weatherizing and one that you would only do if you own your home, in which case it will offer a return on your investment by saving on your energy bill. Many utility companies around the country offer free energy analysis services and discounts for insulation. It takes a professional only half a day to insulate the attic of a 2,000-square-foot home with blown-in cellulose insulation, and it will cost around $300 to $400. Studies have shown that by combining weather stripping and insulation the average house could cut its energy needs by 30 percent. When you're counting every drop of gas or degree of heat, it can make a tremendous difference.

3. Lighting   Lighting alone eats up 20 percent of the electricity used in this country, equaling the energy produced by all the nuclear reactors put together. Keep that in mind the next time you are pondering how many lights to leave on in your home when heading out for dinner and a movie. Lamps soak up a lot of juice!

Start saving energy today by replacing incandescent bulbs with some compact *fluorescent* lightbulbs. They are a must! People are often put off by the heftier up-front cost of fluorescent bulbs ($6.50-$16 at Home Depot and other home centers), compared to regular incandescent bulbs ($1 at the most). However, fluorescent bulbs more than make up for the cost with their extremely long life and energy savings. It's estimated that you can save between $30 to $60 on energy over the life of the bulb without sacrificing lighting quality. This is the kind of habit you can easily change now before Y2K.

If you're wondering how lightbulbs can help you prepare for possible power outages, you're paying attention. If you buy a generator or battery/inverter system to prepare for a Y2K power failure, every watt that you use counts.

For an emergency situation, compact fluorescent bulbs dramatically reduce the energy drain on your battery inverter system or generator while increasing the length of time you can use a lamp by five times for the same amount of light!

The renewable resource suppliers have the biggest selection of these bulbs (*See Real Goods or Jade Mountain on page 184.*), but Home Depot has a pretty good inventory, too.

Fluorescent bulb

Courtesy of Real Goods

The chart below shows how compact fluorescent bulbs use only a fraction of wattage as compared to typical incandescent bulbs for about five times the light. For example, a 13-watt fluorescent bulb will produce light comparable to a 60-watt regular bulb.

Bulb Types with Comparable Lighting

Compact Fluorescent		Typical Incandescent
5 watt	=	25 watt
7 watt	=	40 watt
10 watt	=	50 watt
13 watt	=	60 watt
18 watt	=	75 watt
22 watt	=	100 watt
26 watt	=	120 watt

NOTE—AC (alternating current) Compact Fluorescent bulbs are not adjustable. Do not operate an AC Compact Fluorescent bulb with a dimmer lighting switch as the switch could overheat and catch fire.

B. Alternative Power Supplies

This chapter helps you prepare for the things impacted most by the lack of electricity and focus on essentials for survival and basic comfort for your family including heating, cooking, and lighting.

When people anticipate preparing for an emergency, they'll often say, "Well, I'll just get a generator." In reading through the generator section, and the rest of the chapter, you may find generators are *not* the best solution for your family, depending on your needs and living situation.

Besides generators, deep-cycle batteries and battery inverters can be used in combination with a generator, which increases its efficiency. In addition, batteries and AC inverters that can supply power independent of a generator by using a solar panel for recharging. Though most battery systems can't take on a lot of wattage, they can handle many small jobs like running a small television, lamp or radio. They're clean, safe, and with solar panels, provide a renewable source of power. In addition, there are longer term strategies to handle your energy needs entirely with solar energy.

Read the entire chapter thoroughly before deciding what's best for your family. You may find some options you had not thought of. There are three basic categories of alternative power supplies to consider:

1. **Generators**
2. **Batteries and Battery Inverters**
3. **Solar Energy**

1. Generators Before you fork over hundreds or even thousands of dollars for a gas generator to prepare for a Y2K power outage, let's discuss some pros and cons. If you've already decided you have *no interest* in acquiring a generator, then you might want to skip to the section on batteries. For those of you considering generators, the following information should make you a smart, savvy consumer.

A gas generator is not practical, economical, or efficient for the person who sees it as their own ready-made electric power company. Most people cannot afford a generator capable of supplying anything close to the tremendous amount of power you normally receive from the local utility company. So hold off on scheduling that January 2000 Super Bowl party with the big-screen TV.

People are often disappointed when they find out their expensive generator runs only a few appliances. For example, a 300-watt generator will run for around nine hours per gallon and operate only a couple of, items like a small TV and a couple of lamps. A large 4,000-watt generator will need a gallon every three hours or so. That means to run a refrigerator and other large appliances, you'd need eight gallons a day or over fifty gallons a week. It is best to forgo the refrigerator.

Another shortfall to generators is fuel storage. Gasoline has a short shelf life (two months maximum), restricting the amount of fuel you can keep on hand. In most residential areas it's illegal to store gasoline because it's so dangerous. Check your local codes before storing gasoline. Also, keep in mind that there's nothing like a loud gas generator to advertise to the world that you have power.

If you still want the security of owning a generator (and it's physically and legally feasible), it can certainly enhance your Y2K preparedness. In addition to providing power for limited living needs, they can provide an energy source to recharge batteries and battery power systems. If you happen to own one already, plan for fuel provisions. Before you purchase a generator, review your options with a dealer. A propane-powered generator is better than one that runs on gasoline. Propane generators are preferable since propane doesn't deteriorate as quickly as gasoline and is relatively inexpensive. However, it's stored in a pressurized tank so you can't refill it with liquid fuel.

Another factor to consider is maintenance. Like any engine, generators need regular checkups—for oil, gas, and air filters. Review the manual for directions on proper maintenance and safety. Make sure you have some extra supplies on hand for maintaining your generator.

Generator Maintenance Tips

1) Change the oil regularly. Follow manufacturer's recommendations.
2) Air filters will typically last two to three years if the generator is not exposed to excessive dirt. Check it from time to time.
3) Before storing a generator, drain all the gas in it. Otherwise, you risk damaging the internal workings of the machine from bad gas.

In order to select a generator that will fit your needs, evaluate what you will use it for. Prioritize your electrical items and appliances so that you can pick and choose items to be powered at any given time. (*See Generator Wattage Chart on page 77.*) Movie buffs who have seen *Apollo 13* can appreciate this: Just as the astronaut kept powering up systems in the mock capsule to see if he could find a way to operate all life-essential systems without exceeding the available power, you too will have limited power with your generator. To confirm the power requirements of each of the items you want to run, look at the information panel usually found on the bottom or back of the appliance or tool. If wattage is not shown, you can calculate it by multiplying the amps times the volts (Amps x Volts = Watts).

Generators run more efficiently if you only draw around half of their generating capability. A good rule of thumb is that you need a generator to provide double the wattage that you actually need for your total use.

Examples:

4,000-watt generator costs around $700
Provides 2,000 useable watts for appliances
About 3.25 hours of service per gallon of fuel

10,000-watt generator costs around $1,900
Provides 5,000 useable watts for appliances
About 2 hours of service per gallon of fuel

For about $250 you can buy a two-outlet, 850-watt generator that might power one or two light fixtures and a radio or TV. (Remember: Be sure to get compact fluorescent bulbs for significant wattage reduction.) Generators can be purchased at most home centers or look in the yellow pages under "Generators-Electric" for a local dealer. You'll also need some heavy-duty extension cords at about $20 each to plug your appliances and other electrical items into the generator. Since the generator should only be used outdoors, you'll need some way to pull the extension cord through. Cracking a door or window will drain precious heat from your home.

Since generators are rated to produce a set amount of power or wattage, to maximize its efficiency you want to use it at its full capacity whenever it's running, or you're wasting the energy its generating. This means that if the generator produces 2,000 useable watts but you're only using 1,200, you're wasting 800 watts and precious fuel. You need to "micromanage" the timing of each item you want to use. For example, if you've powered up the generator to use a computer and printer (estimated 355 watts), a television (170 watts) and a radio (between 50 and 200 watts), but then you finish with the computer and the generator is still running for the other items, you end up burning more energy (and fuel) than you're using. This kind of waste is important to minimize when dealing with any type of long-term emergency. Managing your power usage will becomes part of your daily reality.

To get the most out of a generator, it's best if you use it in combination with a battery and AC inverter system. The generator charges up the battery as it's operating so the battery can store power for later use. This way, you get the maximum benefit from the energy that the generator produces with little waste.

These appliance and equipment ratings are estimates and should only be used as a rough guide. Confirm the power requirements of each of the items you will run by looking directly on the appliance. If wattage is not shown, you can calculate it by multiplying the amps times the volts.

(Amps x Volts = Watts).

Generator Wattage Chart

Appliance	Running Watts	Appliance	Running Watts
Air conditioner (10k Btu)	1500/ton	Blender	350
Clothes dryer (electric)	5750	Clothes dryer (gas)	500
Coffee maker	1200	Computer (Laptop)	50
Dishwasher	500	14" Color Monitor	100
Freezer	500	Furnace fan	700
Garage door 1/2 hp	600	Hair dryer	1000
Iron	1200	Lamps & lighting	500
Dishwasher	40-200	Microwave oven	1200
Radio/stereo	50-200	Refrigerator/freezer	1000
Space heater	1300	Range, sm. burner	1250
Tape/CD player	50	25" Television	170
VCR	30	19" TV	80
Toaster	900-1500	Vacuum cleaner-average	900
Washing machine	1200	Water heater	3500
Air compressor 1 hp	1000	Air compressor 1-1/2 hp	1600

Generator Wattage Chart (*continued*)

Tools	Running Watts	Tools	Running Watts
Air compressor 1 hp	1000	Air compressor 1-1/2 hp	1600
Airless sprayer 3/4 hp	850	Battery charger	120
1 hand drill 1/2"	650	Router	1100
Sander, 3x24" belt	1200	Saw, chain	1000
Saw, 7-1/4" circular	1560	Saw, jig	500
Saw, orbital	300	Saw, radial arm	1200

GASOLINE WARNING

If you have a gas generator, be aware that gasoline is very dangerous and doesn't store very long. With all its additives and chemical compounds, gas is very unstable and only has a shelf life of about two months. If you talk to your local lawnmower repairman, he'll probably tell you that a big chunk of his business is fixing carburetors gummed up by bad gas. If the generator runs out of fuel while operating, read the instruction manual to see if it is safe to refuel while hot. Refueling can be very dangerous.

When storing gas, always keep it away from your home. Even your garage is not considered safe. Also, many cities do not allow gas storage in residential areas so you should check on that. Gas that has gone bad needs to be dumped at a hazardous materials dumping site.

2. Batteries and Battery Inverters When you start looking into the possibilities of power disruptions, you'll probably discover more about batteries than you ever dreamed of. Fortunately, you might be impressed with what you find. Batteries are basically receptacles for electrical power which makes them well-suited for emergency backup purposes. Like a gas tank or a carton of milk, once a battery is full, it's full. You cannot recharge it beyond its capacity.

Batteries have been around for one hundred years, and the technology hasn't changed much. In the world of boaters and RV users, batteries have long been the heart of their free-standing energy systems. However, boats and RVs have a built-in method of recharging their batteries—their engines. These aren't the kind of batteries that go in a flashlight; these are called "Deep-Cycle Batteries." Many of them look more like a car battery, although they come in larger sizes, too. (*See "A Valuable Lesson on Batteries" on page 112 for information about regular appliance batteries.*) For emergency purposes, you must have a way to recharge the battery to get ongoing use out of them beyond a day or two. The best methods to do this are:

- **A generator**—Simply plug the battery into the generator to recharge it.
- **A solar panel**—Solar panels are one of the greatest inventions of this decade.

With the ability to convert sunlight into electricity, solar panels provide a safe, quiet, and environmentally clean source of energy. A solar panel powerful enough to recharge a battery in one day of sun will run you about $300. These can be ordered from a renewable energy supplier like Jade Mountain or Real Goods. (*See page 184.*) Obviously, if you live in a northern climate where sun is limited this is not practical for Y2K preparedness, but for those in sunnier climates, a battery and inverter kit with a solar panel could be a great emergency backup solution to operate a few small appliances.

If you compare a solar panel and battery system to using a generator, the up-front cost, based on similar power capabilities, may be about the same as a generator but, in the long run, the solar system could provide savings if you continue to use the solar panel. There are no moving parts on a solar panel, so it's not going to wear out like a generator, and it doesn't need gasoline. For Y2K problems, the ideal way to keep a consistent supply of power would be to have an extra battery that is always recharging with the solar panel. Then just rotate the recharged one around as the one in use gets depleted.

Battery Power:

   a. **Car**
   b. **True Deep-Cycle**
   c. **Marine or RV Deep-Cycle**

   a. Car Batteries   Car batteries are not meant for this kind of remote power source because they are designed only for quick-start service for your car and then are recharged as you drive. They should not be cycled down more than 10 percent of their capacity: If they are, the life of the battery is dramatically reduced. Also, they are not meant to be handled and should never be brought indoors because they produce toxic fumes and can leak battery acid. They can also explode. A car battery should be used for auxiliary power *only in a serious emergency.*

   b. True Deep-Cycle Batteries   These batteries are also referred to as "golf cart batteries" and are the best choice for emergency purposes and long-term battery investment. According to Real Good's *Solar Living Sourcebook*, these batteries are built to handle hundreds, if not thousands of charges. They last longest if they are used only down to 50 percent capacity between charges, giving them a 220 amp-hour rating or eleven amps for twenty hours. Actual performance, however, depends on factors including location, temperature, and use. The life expectancy of a typical "golf cart" battery can be from three to five years and up to fifteen to twenty years for the Industrial Chloride forklift-type batteries.

   c. Marine or RV Deep Cycle Batteries   Often referred to as deep-cycle batteries, these twelve-volt batteries are designed to be recharged frequently from the engine of a boat or RV, but they have a lesser capacity than a true deep-cycle battery of between 80 and 160 amp-hours and a shorter life expectancy of two to three years.

Battery Inverters

Battery inverters, in combination with the rechargeable batteries, complete your back-up power supply. The inverters are small, ugly little boxes that plug into the battery to convert the battery's DC (Direct Current) power to AC (Alternating Current) power so you can operate things in your home like TVs, lamps, computers, and radios. The inverters have a DC outlet on one side, to plug into the battery, and an AC outlet on the other, to plug these appliances into.

   Inverters come in different wattage outputs and are sized according to their maximum wattage output at any one time. Obviously, the more powerful the battery is and the greater wattage capacity of the inverter, the more use you can get out of the system. For example, if you are watching a TV that uses 35 watts and have a reading light that uses 60 watts, you would need to use an inverter that provides at least 95 watts. It is always recommended to slightly oversize inverters to account for conversion losses. Thus choosing at least a 110-watt or higher inverter would be minimal to run those two items. The price of inverters rises with the capacity, starting at around $80 for a small 100-watt inverter, $300 for a 500-watt inverter and $800 for a 1,500-watt inverter.

Battery inverters are excellent choices due to recent techno-logical advances. Of course, these are not the perfect answer to all power outages because you're still limited by the capacity of the battery, the power of the inverter, and the power needs of what-ever you want to operate. Also, you must factor in how you will recharge your battery and how long that will take. Nonetheless, given their benefits, it may be worth looking into for Y2K backup energy preparedness. To learn more about what would best serve your specific needs and budget, read some of the books available on alternative energy options and talk to an alternative energy supplier listed on page 184.

Battery Backup Option

To add to your pile of emergency toys, there is a small, easy-to-use plug-and-play battery and inverter system ready-made for emer-gency use—and at a great price! It's called the Porta-Power Boost It Pack ($150). In tests, a lamp with a compact fluorescent bulb and a radio/CD player ran for over six hours with no trouble at all. For use after Y2K, Porta-Power is ideal for camping or roadside emergencies and powerful enough to jump-start a dead battery. The unit has an easy-carry handle and built-in plug for recharging from a generator or a solar panel. (In normal conditions, you can recharge on your AC current at home.) It may be best to use solar energy to recharge Porta-Power Boost It Pack.

Courtesy of Sun Solor Systems

To get the best use of this, or any, battery and in-verter package, you will want a solar panel powerful enough to recharge the battery in one day so that you can more reliably

Porta-Power Boost It Pack

count on being able to use the system at night. This way you set up a system of rotation—charging during the day, then using the power at night.

Certainly, when charging your Power Pack up by the sun, you need to take into consideration the available "full" sunlight in your area. For instance, if you are using a 49-watt solar, that panel will recharge the Power Pack battery at about 49 watts of electricity per hour of "full" sunlight. If you have an average of four hours of "full" sunlight per day in your area, then the above-mentioned panel will recharge the battery with about 196 watts. The panel would almost completely recharge the battery pack in one day under these sunny conditions. This size solar panel costs around $300 including a voltage regulator. The voltage regulator is important because without one, the solar panels can damage the electronic equipment inside the Porta-Power Boost It Pack and the battery itself.

There are less expensive solar panels in the $100 to $150 range, but these types take around two to three days to recharge the battery. (For complete product information see www.webaccess.net/~sunsolarsystems on the Internet.)

Courtesy of Sun Solar Systems

Porta-Power Boost It Pack in use

110/120-Volt AC Accessories Powered By
Boost It & Power Inverter

Accessory	Wattage Consumption/ Continuous	Full Battery Charge
Cordless Drill Charger 7 Volts	15 Watts	9 Hours
Camcorder Charger 6-Volts	25 Watts	3 Hours & 20 Min.
Cellular Phone Charger	30 Watts	3 Hours & 15 Min.
VCR	45 Watts	2 Hours & 15 Min.
CD Charger	65 Watts	2 Hours
13" Color TV	70 Watts	2 Hours
Laptop Computer	90 Watts	1 Hour & 45 Min.
Work Light	100 Watts	1 Hour & 30 Min.
20" Color TV/VCR	120 Watts	55 Min.
Soldering Gun	135 Watts	50 Min.
27" Color TV	160 Watts	55 Min.
Fax Machine	170 Watts	50 Min.
Am/Fm Stereo	210 Watts	40 Min.
Jig Saw	235 Watts	30 Min.
Spot Light/Work Light	250 Watts	25 Min.

The wattages in this chart are generic. Some brands exceed the wattages listed. Before using your accessories, refer to the owner's manual for actual wattage required.

NOTE: Estimated working time is based on the BOOST IT unit at full charge. For 110/120 Volt-rated appliances, a power inverter must be used with the BOOST IT power pack. Select an inverter with a higher continuous wattage capacity than the device you want to operate.

3. Solar Energy   As our most abundant and renewable resource of energy, solar energy must be included in the mix as an option for alternative energy. The previous section touched on solar energy, this one explores it in depth.

Heating space and water are the largest devourers of electricity. Michael Potts, an expert in self-sustainable living, calls hot water heating particularly offensive. "Our conventional water heaters maintain dozens of gallons of water at a piping hot temperature twenty-four hours a day, just in case someone needs a teaspoon full," Potts says, "(This) is particularly difficult to justify when we consider that solar domestic hot water systems are efficient and easy to install and operate."

What if there were a way to generate all your own power affordably without adding to the contamination of the planet at the same time? Great advances in state-of-the-art solar technology make it possible to provide a viable energy alternative to meet your family's needs, as well as a tangible solution to environmental problems caused by pollution. Potts points out that the southern regions of the United States provide an ideal climate for solar-power generation; nonetheless, some of the finest examples of successful solar homes are in the Rockies, where winter days are bright and reflect light off snowfall, amplifying the intensity of the sun for increased power to the solar panels.

As awareness of the effectiveness of solar energy grows, there may be an increase in the number of people "harvesting" energy for at least some of their needs. In fact, many people, like John Schaeffer (president of Real Goods Trading Company) and his family, have developed what they call a "solar conservation power plant" that allows them to sell unused energy back to their local utility company. "An integral part of this change will be net metering, which means that the electricity we generate and that which we consume sells for the same price," says Potts.

You might find that a long-term investment strategy in solar power makes sense—Y2K or no Y2K. If you're purchasing emergency backup equipment anyway, such as deep-cycle batteries and inverters, you could apply these things to an overall self-sustainable solar energy system that would not only deal with the Y2K crisis but could also serve you well into the next century.

There are many things to evaluate when considering a solar system. Because installing solar panels costs thousands of dollars, the return on the investment must be amortized over many years. If you plan to move out of your home in less than five years, then installation of equipment that you can't take with you probably isn't a good idea. The exact timetable to see a return is based on highly variable and individual circumstances such as: How much sun do you get? how extensive is your system? what's the overall energy efficiency of your home? You should expect it to take ten to fifteen years for an alternative energy system to pay for itself.

This section is not intended to be a complete discussion on solar energy but is an invitation to learn more about this extraordinary and powerful energy resource. In addition to solar power, explore the possibilities of wind power and hydropower as part of an overall self-sustainable home. There are many books available on these subjects, and the suppliers listed in the back can help you with specific questions. For clear and concise explanations of solar living, check out Michael Potts's book *The Independent Home— Living Well with Power from the Sun, Wind and Water* and Real Goods' *Solar Living Sourcebook*.

If preparing for Y2K is the motivation you've needed to take a larger view of your energy investment and to consider incorporating a more independent self-sustaining system such as solar into your home, then there are some positive benefits of the Y2K crisis.

C. Heating, Cooking, and Lighting

Let's return to the basics of life and what you will need to consider if and when the perils of Y2K hit and send you straight back into the nineteenth century, where wood stoves, oil lamps, and carrying water from a nearby well or stream ruled the day. Start by thinking of all this as an extended camping trip (attitude is important), especially when it comes to cooking, heating, and lighting—without RV hookups, if you hadn't already figured that out! Let's take each of these areas one at a time, starting with heat because you're probably going to be cold quicker than you'll be hungry.

1. Heating   Once you get over your disbelief about the consequences of Y2K failures, it doesn't take long to realize that January 1, 2000, falls in the dead of winter, at least for residents of either North America or Europe. Staying warm through possible power failures becomes a central issue for many of us.

There are various heating options depending on where you live and what kind of living space you have:

a. **Fireplaces**
b. **Woodstoves**
c. **Gas stoves**
d. **Kerosene heaters**

a. Fireplaces   Sing around the campfire? It's hard to beat a fireplace to create a cozy and inviting atmosphere, right? Well, yes, if ambiance is all you're looking for. Unfortunately, the garden variety fireplace can cause negative heat efficiency. That means, you could be losing heat from your home up the chimney flue. At best, a regular fireplace is only 20 percent efficient.

To increase efficiency to over 90 percent, consider installing a ventless gas log with propane gas. If you already have a fireplace, this is a good source of heat for a minimal amount of preparation. They put out so much heat (38,000 Btus), you can't sit near it comfortably for very long. With these, you only need to have your chimney damper open about a quarter inch for ventilation.

As with any gas unit, gas logs need to be installed by a certified propane (LP) installer. Get a referral from your local dealer or look in the phone book under "Gas-Propane."

b. Woodstoves   Freestanding woodstoves are another way to go for heating. Regardless of what happens with the Y2K crisis, woodstoves have long been a low-tech heat source of choice for those living in rural areas with access to large amounts of wood. If you don't already have a woodstove, these require some effort and/or money to install.

If a woodstove is your choice, evaluate your space requirements. They must be placed at least thirty inches from any combustible surface such as a house wall. Otherwise, you can install a heat shield that mounts on the back of the stove (it costs about $70), allowing you to get six inches from the wall. You'll also want to lay some kind of fireproof flooring under and around the woodstove, such as tile or brick.

Unless you're pretty handy and own a lot of tools, you'll probably need to have the unit professionally installed, since the flue has to be cut through the roof. Also available are woodstove inserts that work the same as a regular unit but backs into the fireplace and draws up the existing chimney. Inserts are about 80 percent efficient.

Finally, don't forget the wood! There's nothing quite like splitting wood, carrying it in to the hearth, and stoking a warm fire or stove. After all, many people spend big bucks and use their vacation time to head out to a log cabin or ski lodge with a fireplace or woodstove to cozy up to: Now you can create the same ambiance in the convenience of your den or living room. Who knows, building fires might be one way you discover a way of life that's pretty wonderful.

Since there are so many varieties of woodstoves, contact a good local retailer who can help walk you through your specific situation. Look under "Stoves-heating" or "Fireplaces" in the Yellow Pages. Different brands, styles, and features affect the price, so you'll need to shop around before making a decision based on your conditions, needs, and budget. The World Wide Web is also a good resource to learn about different brands and features.

c. Gas Stoves There have been many fantastic advances in gas space heaters that provide a viable and reasonably priced alternative to woodstoves or gas fireplaces.

Vent-free propane heaters offer high energy efficiency, thermostatic controls, matchless ignitions, and the latest in gas technology. They are available in a wide range of styles and types including wall-mounted or free-

Vent-free gas stove

standing models. Some gas heaters give a "fireplace" appearance; others have the character and look of an old-fashioned woodstove. Just because it's preparedness doesn't mean it has to be ugly. (Look out Martha Stewart!)

Prices for a vent-free unit start at around $225 (without a thermostat), $315 (with a thermostat), and on up to well over $1,000 for the fancy hand-finished, cast-iron models with all the European styling or country charm you could ever want. The Jade Mountain Catalog has several models, and they can help you decide what's best for you. You can also call your local heating/fireplace dealer or do computer research.

Vent-free heaters should be professionally installed. You should never keep a propane gas tank in your home so, you need to run gas lines from the bulk tank outside to the heater inside.

Propane Fuel

Propane appliances make good sense for your Y2K investment dollar for many reasons. Propane is cheap and, just as important, it is also a lot safer to use than gas and easier to store. Since it is kept in pressurized tanks, you don't have to handle raw fuel or expose yourself to dangerous fumes that could explode due to a spark.

Because it keeps longer than gas, you could store a two-year supply of propane in a 500-gallon tank. Versatility is a major selling point for propane, too. It is a flexible energy source that can be used for other equipment like propane lanterns, cookstoves, and generators, so you can make the most of your gas supply. If you want to really go all out, you can even get propane refrigerators for up to $2,000.

Figure out how large a propane tank you want, based on how much you think you'll use the heater or other appliances. For very short-term emergency preparedness, you could get by with a twenty-pound tank from Sears for around $26. Then, you can fill the tank for $8 to $10 at a local gas station that handles propane. For all your trouble though, a larger size—either a thirty-pound tank (about $55 full) or a forty-pound tank ($60 full)—may be better. That way you're covered for a longer period in case Y2K power breakdowns persist, yet the tanks aren't so big that you can't move them if needed. Never store a tank inside.

To purchase the larger propane tanks or buy the propane gas itself, call your local propane dealer, and they will be happy to help you. Shop around since prices can vary. (Look in your phone book under "Gas-Propane" for a dealer nearest you.)

It's impossible to make flat statements about how long a tank of fuel will last with all the variables of room size, house insulation, and desired heat intensity. However, to give you a rough idea, propane fuel will provide an average of ten to twenty hours of heat service from one gallon at 99 percent efficiency. That's a lot of heat for the money figuring on about $12 to fill a 40-gallon tank. (For you techies, or even Trekkies, propane has an energy content of 92,700 Btus per gallon.)

The benefits of propane fuel are numerous:

- Reasonable cost, good value
- Safer then gas, no fuel handling
- Far longer storage than gas
- Clean and efficient burning

- Odor-free
- Versatile

You should be aware that any kind of vent-free heating unit burns off oxygen as it produces heat and thereby creates carbon monoxide. Good quality gas heaters come with ODS Sensors (Oxygen Depletion Sensors) built in and will automatically turn the heater off if the oxygen level gets too low.

It's good to know that generally, home gas heaters are considered safe in typical homes, meaning homes that are not unusually tight against air infiltration. In these common conditions, there is an adequate supply of air for combustion and ventilation through normal infiltration. If you use the heater in a room smaller than 200 square feet, you must keep a door to an adjacent room open or a window opened at least one inch. Also, do not use a gas-heat unit in a bathroom or other small room with the door closed.

d. Kerosene Heaters These have been around for a long time and are probably the lowest-cost option next to wool blankets and down sleeping bags. One of the most widely available brands is the Kero-son kerosene heaters that you can find at Sears and other major merchandisers for about $150. You can even get a kerosene combo heater/cookstove unit for around $100 (Major Surplus and Survival carries them. Call 800-441-8855.)

Kerosene heaters require more maintenance and are not as safe as the propane heaters since the heater requires a wick to burn and must be refueled directly into the heater's fuel tank. Refilling the fuel tank should *never* be done when the heater is hot. In addition, they do not come with an ODS (Oxygen Depletion Sensor), so you have to rely on battery-operated carbon monoxide detectors and your own good sense. Following are some vitally important dos and don'ts regarding kerosene heaters:

- *Never use gasoline.*
- Never store kerosene in a *red* container (these indicate *gas*).

- Never refill with fuel while the heater is hot and never indoors—always outdoors.
- Read the safety manual carefully.
- *Always* keep battery-operated carbon monoxide detectors and smoke detectors in good working order. (Find them at Kmart, Wal-Mart, Costco and others.) You can install them as separate units or find one unit that does both. (These are also good to use with gas lanterns.)

In addition to storing extra fuel, the kerosene heaters require a wick, so be sure to have extra wicks on hand. If you lose power and don't have a wick for your heater, all you'll have is an expensive gas container.

Fuel efficiency varies with the efficiency of the kerosene heating unit and the level of use. For example, the Kero-son Omni 230 holds almost two gallons with a burn time of twelve to sixteen hours. This translates into one or two gallons a day of fuel to store, depending on whether you're using the heater most of the day or at night only. I suggest you store *at least* two to four weeks' worth of kerosene. Some Y2K experts believe that if the power grid goes down in various regions, Herculean efforts would be made to restore power to at least the large urban areas within two weeks. There's little doubt that the more-populated areas will be the biggest priority, so if you live in a more remote area, you should be prepared to handle your own needs for at least a month.

Other Thoughts on Heating

Remember, fuel efficiency is important if Y2K power problems drag on, so try to minimize use during the day by staying active and dressing warmly. Think layers—fleece shirts, down vests, wool sweaters. Have plenty of extra blankets around, and take this time as an opportunity to buy that handsome down or wool coat you've been wanting. You may really need it!

If there are people in your household with special needs, like a new baby, elderly folks, or someone with special medical needs, investigate your neighborhood, your church, or your local Y2K community group for resources. (These groups are springing up in cities and towns all over the country.) The Cassandra Project Web site (www.cassandraproject.org) keeps a list of local community groups throughout the United States with contact phone numbers and e-mail addresses. Also, keep an eye out in your local paper for announcements of Y2K meetings in your area.

So far, you've been fed a lot of condensed information about various heating options available to you in lieu of electrically powered sources. There is no preferred heating option suitable for everyone across the country, so it's up to you to decide what is most feasible and effective for your specific needs and finances. In the meantime, however, ask yourself the following questions and come up with honest answers applicable to you and your family. There should be enough information provided earlier in this chapter for you to make informed decisions:

- Should I go with wood or gas?
- How much will the system cost?
- How much will it cost to install?

For woodstoves:

- Where should I install the woodstove and do I have enough floor space to allow for fire code safety requirements?
- Do I need a fire shield so I can place the stove closer to a wall?
- What is the cost of the flue?
- Don't forget to add the cost of fireproof floor treatment.

For gas heaters:

- Is this heater strictly for emergency backup or should I spend more for an auxiliary system that I could use regularly?
- Is the room large enough to properly ventilate?
- Will I be using other propane appliances, too? If so, how big a propane tank should I get?

Stoves	Btus	Efficiency	Fuel/Safety	Cost
Fireplace	N/A	20%	Wood/Very	N/A
Ventless Gas Logs	38,000	90%	Propane/Good	$300-400
Woodstoves	N/A	80%	Wood/Very	$800-1,500
Gas Stoves	92,700 per/gal.	90%+	Propane/Good	$225-1,000
Kerosene Heaters	23,000	N/A	Kerosene/Moderate	$100-150

2. Cooking If you think of cooking in a Y2K crisis as a camp out in your house, you're home free. Fact is, you and anyone else living with you are going to need to consume three meals a day for the duration, and it's inconceivable that you're going to make it all the way through with prepared food that doesn't need to be at least heated, let alone cooked. A diet of Twinkies, yesterday's donuts, bags of potato chips, and soda pop isn't going to cut it— not beyond twenty-four hours, anyway. Without electricity to power up your stove and refrigerator, you're going to need to improvise when it comes to cooking. When choosing cooking implements consider cost, ease of use, and type of fuel used. Here are the main options for emergency cooking preparedness:

a. **Camping Gas Stoves**
b. **Other Quick Emergency Options**
c. **Solar Ovens**
d. **Refrigeration**

a. Camping Gas Stoves If you've ever gone camping with bad coffee and lumpy oatmeal, then you should be familiar with the two-burner gas stoves. (But you can't blame the stove for the lousy food!) For Y2K preparedness, look for a stove that's going to give you the greatest emergency flexibility. After that, you can look at ease of use.

Dual-Fuel Stoves Since our focus is on emergency preparedness, not camping or backpacking, emergency experts say that the best choice is a dual-fuel camp stove. (They cost from $50 to $100.) The Coleman Powerhouse dual-fuel, two-burner unit (or three-burner model) runs on Coleman fuel *or* unleaded gasoline. This way, if power problems persist over several days or even weeks, raw fuel, such as gasoline, is more likely to be available, even during supply shortages.

The dual-fuel stoves cost more than the propane ones, but you have to factor in the possibility that you could quickly run out of the disposable propane bottles. (As an example, I talked to a Sears salesman in Florida who told me that even the slightest threat of a hurricane quickly cleared the propane bottles off shelves everywhere.) However, if you already have a propane tank,

Dual-Fuel Stove

Courtesy of the Coleman Company

you have the option of converting the stove to propane. To do this, you must purchase a simple propane adapter kit, not made by Coleman, but designed for their stoves.

The best thing to do is to stick to the Coleman brand of fuel if you can. It burns clean and the biggest advantage is that it can be stored up to a few years in an unopened can and up to one year once the can has been opened. However, if all you have is gasoline, Coleman has refined its dual-fuel stove to provide excellent performance with unleaded auto gas, perfect for emergency situations. For instance, you could drain gas from your car's tank or lawn mower, if you had to. These stoves have been specially engineered to accommodate automobile gas, which has more impurities that can clog your stove than Coleman fuel. This also means that if your stove is not designed for unleaded gas, don't use gas unless you absolutely have to, or you will quickly reduce its life span and performance. That goes for dual-fuel lanterns, too.

Extra supplies you will need include a spare generator ($15 to $20) for your stove. This isn't the generator with motors, but a simple brass device that delivers fuel to the stove's heating element. They can get clogged up eventually over long periods of use. And Lou Malin at Major Surplus & Supply and resident preparedness expert strongly recommends that you get a "sparker" that mounts inside your gas stove. He says "they'll save your match supply, which is important when you're dealing with emergency conditions." Sparkers come as a separate attachment and are available in camping stores.

Coleman stoves are readily available at sporting goods stores and mass merchandisers such as Wal-Mart, Target, Sears, and others. Primas Stoves is another quality brand of two- and three-burner stoves available at REI, the national sporting goods chain (www.rei.com or 800-426-4800). Most camping stores also carry single-burner lightweight portable stoves if you want to invest in something that you could use later for backpacking trips.

Remember, any gas-burning device must be operated in a ventilated area. When cooking with any stove like this, keep a window slightly open to let fresh air in. Next, let's review some advantages and disadvantages of the dual-fuel stoves.

Advantages:

- Best solution for emergency preparedness since liquid fuels are more readily available in emergency situations.
- Coleman fuels have much longer shelf life than unleaded gasoline, but you can use gasoline, if necessary.
- Liquid fuels are much cheaper than disposable propane bottles.
- Provides additional emergency heat source (*ventilate the area*).
- Can be adapted to using a propane tank if that is the preferred fuel source (adapter kit must be purchased separately).
- Products are durable and can provide service for many years.

Disadvantages:

- Fuel tanks cannot be refilled when hot to touch and must be filled outdoors.
- Fuel can spill, increasing danger and waste.
- Fuel tank must be primed.
- Must be ventilated to the outdoors, which will cause some heat loss.

Propane Stoves   Propane stoves are cheaper than dual-fuel stoves. Propane is easier to use. If you already have a propane tank, you can purchase an adapter and long hose that allows you to connect the stove to a bulk propane tank (twenty-gallon, forty-gallon, and up) rather than using more expensive, disposable propane bottles. If you have to, you could also cook with your outdoor gas grill that usually comes with a twenty-gallon propane tank. But leave it outside! (For more information on propane and propane tanks, see the previous Heating section.)

If you stick with the propane bottles, just be sure to have plenty on hand—you only get about four to five hours of use from one bottle. You can stretch the efficiency of the fuel by not operating the burners at their hottest. Let's review some advantages and disadvantages of the propane stoves:

Advantages:

- Propane burns cleaner than gasoline.
- You can tap into existing propane tanks, if you have them.
- They are cheaper than dual-fuel stoves.

Disadvantages:

- In a bind you cannot resort to using gasoline.
- Must be ventilated to the outdoors, which will cause some heat loss.

A Reminder: You should not store or cook with any size propane tank in your house. Lou Malin of Major Surplus and Supply says, "I can't imagine someone being stupid enough to bring their gas grill barbecue in the house."

Kerosene Stoves   These are an old standard for cooking. You can even get a combo kerosene cooker/heating unit for stovetop cooking. Kerosene is less volatile than gas or propane, so when spilled it doesn't evaporate or ignite easily. Kerosene fuel is available all over the world, however it puts out a noticeable gas smell that may bother some people. For the best results, use only grade #1 or deodorized, the highest grade you can get.

Let's review some advantages and disadvantages of kerosene stoves.

Advantages:

- Kerosene is less volatile than gasoline and propane.
- It is readily available.

Disadvantages:

- Kerosene has an odor.
- It doesn't evaporate easily.

Two-burner Gas Camp stove

Period	Fuel Consumed
1 day	4 pints/2 liters
1 week	3.5 gals/13 liters
1 month	14 gals/52 liters
6 months	84 gals/312 liters

Two-burner Propane Stove

Period	Fuel Consumed
1 day	14.6 oz
1 week	6-16.4 oz cylinders
1 month	27 lbs
6 months	8-20 lb tanks

Considering Fuels

Stoves can also provide an additional heat source. But you must provide ventilation whether cooking or heating. Regardless of the type of stove you go with, never leave an open flame unattended, especially with small children around. Also, be sure to have a fire extinguisher handy. Use the small canister ABC type.

Naturally, it's awful to think you could go to all kinds of trouble to have a cookstove and then not have enough fuel. So store enough to last at least two to four weeks. Fuel should be kept in clean, clearly marked containers and placed in a cool location away from open flame or pilot lights. They should never be exposed to heat that exceeds 120 degrees Fahrenheit.

Your selection of a stove may be based to some extent on the kind of fuel supply you want to deal with. For this reason, it may make sense to go with devices like stoves, heaters, and lanterns that all use the same kind of fuel. The best advice is to try to keep the number of different fuels to a minimum. Trying to stay on top of five different kinds of fuels for all your equipment could be a bit of a headache, but face the fact, you'll probably end up with some different kinds of fuels like Coleman fuel for the stove and propane fuel for the heater. That's just the way it is—call it the Y2K juggling act!

Comparing Fuels for Stoves

Stoves	Advantages	Disadvantages
Coleman	Spilled fuel evaporates readily; stove fuel used for priming; highest heat output; best cold weather fuel	Priming sometimes required; spilled fuel very flammable; self-pressuring stoves must be insulated from snow or cold.
Kerosene	Spilled fuel won't ignite readily; fuel sold throughout the world; high heat output.	Priming required; spilled fuel does not evaporate readily; noticeable odor.
Propane/Butane	No-spill fuel container; no priming required; immediate maximum heat output.	Cartridge disposal is a problem; fuel must be kept above freezing for efficient operation**

Comparing Fuels for Stoves (*continued*)

Stoves	Advantages	Disadvantages
Unleaded Auto Gas*	The most readily available fuel in the U.S.; stove fuel used for priming.	Same disadvantages as Coleman. Also, certain gas additives can eventually lead to clogging and corrosion of stove parts.
Solid Fuel	No fuel to pack, no fuel spills.	Can't use in no-fire areas; performance lags behind other fuels.

*Caution, do not use automotive fuel unless specified. Do not use oxygenated gas (found in some places in the U.S. during the winter months).

**Bulk cylinders enable propane stoves to burn efficiently at low temperatures; propane fuel canisters perform much better in low temperatures than butane alone.

b. Other Quick Emergency Options These are other options to keep in mind when all others fail. They are not recommended as the only cooking methods but as backup options to keep in mind for extreme cases.

▸ **Outdoor Grills**—If you have to, you can resort to using your outdoor grill for cooking. However, it's important to realize that in an emergency, it's not likely you'll be able to get a few steaks to throw on the grill for dinner, unless you live in a rural area and have cows or can hunt your own food. Remember, it will be cold in most places so that means you'll be outdoors in freezing temperatures trying to cook. Do not bring your outdoor grill indoors.

▸ **Solid Fuel—Alco-brite (gelled-alcohol fuel)** If you've decided you only want to do the most basic and inexpensive cooking preparedness, you can for a little peace of mind, Alco-brite produces a product made from gelled ethanol that will give safe and reliable service. Alco-brite comes in a small can. To use it, you pry open the lid and light the

Gelled Alcohol, also called Ethanol, which is an organic environmentally safe fuel. It looks like a hard jelly inside and all you do it light it. It lasts for four hours and can boil water in ten minutes or fry an egg in four to five minutes. It won't burn like a camp stove but it's cheap and it works.

It burns very clean as it only gives off CO_2 and water vapor so you can burn it safely indoors. Because the gel is so stiff, there's no troublesome "spill-factor," especially with kids around. When you're finished cooking, turn it off by replacing the lid. The company also claims that one can heat up an average sized room to 65 degrees from freezing.

Alco-brite retails for about $3.50 a can and can be found in camping stores, stove shops, and some Home Depots. Call the Alco-brite company to find a dealer in your area (800-473-0717). You can get a small little utility stove unit (about $19.95) that the Alco-brite can drops into for better cooking stability.

➤ **Fondue pots and other tips** Food can be heated with fondue pots, chafing dishes, and candle warmers. There are long-burning candles made by the Nuwick Company that come in a very wide tin base for stability that you can heat foods with. You can even use a fireplace to cook, if you have one, but as discussed in the heating section, this could result in heat loss through the flue. If necessary, canned food can be eaten right out of the can. If you heat the can, be sure to remove the label, and open the can first.

General Cooking Reminders

Caution: Regardless of the kind of cooking implement you use, always have a fire extinguisher on hand and exercise fire safety.

c. Solar Ovens   They may look like something from another planet, but solar ovens really work! They are designed to receive the sun's rays and amplify its heating powers. And the energy is free!

A solar oven is a great Y2K solution for those of you who live in the southern regions of the United States. Who says you have to give up fresh-baked chocolate chip cookies? Solar ovens commonly reach temperatures of 350 degrees with a mid-range quality unit ($200) and up to 500 degrees for the top of the line unit ($500). They will bake, brown, roast, and boil. (Available through Jade Mountain—*see page 184*.) The Sun Toys Solar Cooker is only $19 and folds into a 14 X 14 X 2-inch packet. Originally designed for camping and backpacking, one fisherman claims he can cook a freshly caught trout in twenty minutes with the Sun Toy Cooker!

Solar oven

Courtesy of Moeb Studios

This technology not only expands your cooking facilities, it doesn't take away from your fuel supply. Also, if overheating is an issue (not everyone will be freezing cold on January 1, 2000), it will keep your kitchen cooler on hot days. Talk to the solar oven dealer to determine whether you get enough sun to make it useful.

Solar ovens have been used in third-world nations for many years. Since 1.4 billion people suffer from cooking fuel shortages, many aid groups from the United States and other countries have shown people all over the world the benefits of cooking food in solar ovens. The savings in wood and the time spent collecting it have had a tremendous impact on these communities. It could make the same difference for your family post-Y2K.

Using a solar oven does mean a significant change in your cooking lifestyle. (Y2K could bring about a change in every aspect of your lifestyle.) Since cooking times are much longer than in a conventional oven, you'll have to prepare meals earlier in the day. For example, if you want a chicken for dinner, you'll have to prepare it in the oven during the day to make use of the sun and allow for a far longer cooking time.

If you want to use a solar oven, start using it right away so you get used to it. Black pots, instead of glass, are recommended for use in a solar oven as thinner pots retain heat better.

d. Refrigeration   Some of you probably believe you can't live without ice cream. Well, it's terrible, but you can and may have to. Refrigeration is something most of us will have to live without if the power goes out. That is why the food chapter focuses on non-perishable and dry foods that don't require refrigeration. If you live in Minnesota or North Dakota, you'll have all the refrigeration you could even ask for but probably no security to keep someone from walking off with your stash.

Don't go to these lengths as it is a luxury in emergency situations, but if you can't bear to live without frozen food, there are some options out there—but they're not cheap:

➡ **Propane refrigerators** Propane refrigerators are available but costly. The smallest ones (2.5 cubic feet) can be purchased for around $550. For an average-sized one, expect to pay between $1,800 and $2,000. You also have to factor in the cost of installing one of the larger propane tanks (500 to 1,000 gallons). If you are retrofitting your home for additional propane appliances like heating and cooking as well, you can spread the cost over these various appliances. If you live in a close-knit community or with a group, you can pool your resources to defray the costs of installing a propane refrigeration system.

➡ **Thermoelectric Coolers** We're all familiar with coolers, but the Coleman Thermoelectric Cooler is different than most. It will plug into a cigarette-lighter jack, or you can get a regular plug-in adapter to use with a generator or battery inverter. (Call the Coleman Company for information (800-835-2703.)

➡ **Regular Coolers** Unless you live in a cold climate these won't be of much use. Still, it's a good idea to stock up on lots of ice on New Year's Eve. If you don't open and close it constantly, a cooler can keep things cold for a good three days.

Dry ice is occasionally mentioned as an alternative to refrigeration, but it's not the best choice. For one thing, it's difficult to handle. It can seriously burn your skin if you touch it. Besides, it's not cheap, it's not readily available, and it only lasts a few days.

C. Lighting

As with all other aspects of this chapter, without electricity lighting is compromised, too. Most of us have experienced temporary
power outages where candles were used to get by. In fact, the first
things most people think of are candles or flashlights, but that's
not good enough for an extended power outage that the Y2K crisis
may bring. Fortunately, there are better options. For a Y2K scenario, power outages could last several days, if not weeks, so
proper emergency preparedness for lighting should be handled
with far safer and longer-lasting devices. Let's take a close look at
the range of options to choose from covering four main categories:

> **1. Gas lanterns**
> **2. Battery lanterns**
> **3. Flashlights**
> **4. Additional backup choices**

   1. Gas Lanterns   For emergency lighting, gas lighting provides the best alternative lighting source if you don't have electrical power. Gas lighting can be broken into three main types: a)
dual-fuel lanterns, b) propane lanterns, and c) kerosene lanterns.
These lanterns come with mantels, which act as the "light bulb"
for the lantern, when you buy the unit. They are very delicate,
and the more you move the lanterns around, the more likely the
mantel will fall apart. For this reason, be sure to stock lots of
extra lantern mantels. Other things to stock up on are extra fuel
tank caps, a glass globe or two for each lantern, and lantern generators. These generators are not the motor kind that you first
think of but are small replaceable brass parts that carry the fuel
to the heating element that get clogged over time. If any one of
these things breaks or gets lost, all you have is a monument to
preparedness.
   Never refill your lantern if it is hot to the touch.

The most significant safety concern to any kind of unvented gas lantern, (or stove as mentioned above) is that they pose a danger of carbon monoxide poisoning, particularly since, unlike a stove, a lamp would typically be used continuously over several hours. Under normal house conditions, in a home not built to air-tight construction standards and heavily insulated, you should be fine using a stove and gas lanterns with good ventilation and slightly opened windows. Let's look at each one in depth.

a. Dual-Fuel Lanterns The best all-around choice for lighting for emergency purposes is the dual-fuel lantern. These will work with either white gas (Coleman fuel) or unleaded gas. You should use unleaded gas in a pinch only. As in the case of the dual-fuel stove, if fuel shortages were to occur, unleaded gas will be the easiest to get. Coleman makes rugged lamps well-suited to emergency purposes and are carried by the mass merchandisers or camping stores. If you use a Coleman lantern, you should stock up on at least two to three gallons of Coleman's own brand of fuel. It stores far longer than gasoline. (See heater/stove section for more informa-tion on the different kinds of gas, including Coleman fuel.)

Unless you have numer-ous lamps, you'll probably find yourself carrying a lantern from room to room—doing things like looking for canned goods on the top shelf of the cabinets, playing games with the kids, or read-ing those books you always said you were going to read. That's okay as long as you're careful. It's best to have

Dual-Fuel Lantern

Courtesy of the Coleman Company

enough lanterns so that you can light more than one room at a time and at the very least enough for the kitchen and main living area.

The dual-fuel lanterns share the same advantages and disadvantages as the dual-fuel stoves but let's review them:

Advantages:

- Good for emergency preparedness since liquid fuels are more readily available and affordable than propane bottles.
- You can use unleaded gasoline, if necessary.
- Liquid fuels are much cheaper than disposable propane bottles.
- Products are durable and can provide service for many years.
- Gas light is brighter than battery lanterns.

Disadvantages:

- Fuel tanks cannot be refilled when hot to touch and must be filled outdoors.
- Fuel can spill, increasing danger and waste.
- Fuel tank must be primed.
- Lantern mantels break easily with lots of movement.
- Must be ventilated to the outdoors, with some heat loss.

Caution: Duel-fuel lantern manufacturers warn against using any fuel lantern indoors due to the danger of carbon monoxide poisoning. *So use at your own risk and ventilate.* Also, *always* install battery-operated carbon monoxide detectors. Test them regularly. *Keep a fire extinguisher on hand.*

---

b. Propane Lanterns Propane lanterns screw into the top of a disposable propane bottle. They're inexpensive at around $14 to $18 plus the cost of the propane bottle and are available at any of the mass merchandisers like Sears, Wal-Mart, Kmart, etc. They put out a decent light, but you're limited to using the propane bottles that you've stored. Once the bottles run out of fuel, that's it. They are not intended for indoor use, although in an emergency you do what you have to do. The advantage to propane lanterns is that they are easier to use than the raw fuel lanterns since you don't have to prime the tank or worry about fuel spillage.

Coleman also makes a "Lantern Tree," which is basically a stalk that attaches to a bulk propane tank. Trouble is, since your tank is placed outdoors, this could only be used for outdoor lighting.

Advantages:

- Propane bottles are easy to operate.
- Propane burns cleaner than other fuels.

Disadvantages:

- Disposable propane bottles cannot be refilled.
- You cannot use other fuels.

All lanterns will run longer if you don't use them on full throttle.

c. Kerosene lanterns The best kerosene lamp around is the Aladdin lamp. Mostly used as indoor lighting, these lamps have been around a long time and are highly efficient. You can get them with glass bases or unbreakable metal bases. Wall brackets can be purchased separately which is a great way to place them out of harm's way, especially with kids around.

Courtesy of Real Goods

Kerosene Lantern

Advantages:

• Kerosene is readily avaiable.
• It is inexpensive.

Disadvantages:

• Kerosene has a strong odor.
• It is not as easy to use as propane.
• You cannot refill kerosene lanterns while hot.

The regular glass kerosene lamp or the barn style hurricane lanterns are okay, too. They're not as efficient as Aladdin's but they're very inexpensive.

Post-Y2K Tip

After Y2K dust settles, hurricane lamps can be filled with citronella fuel to repel insects.

Use outdoors only.

Gas Lamps 6 hrs/day

Period	Fuel Consumed
1 day	1 pint/0.95 liter
1 week	1 gal/4 liters
1 month	4 gals/16 liters
6 months	24 gals/96 liters

Gas Lamps 20 hrs/day

Period	Fuel Consumed
1 day	3 pints/1.5 liters
1 week	2.6 gals/10 liters
1 month	10.4 gals/40 liters
6 months	62 gals/240 liters

Dual Mantel Propane Lamp 6 hrs/day

Period	Fuel Consumed
1 day	8.2 oz
1 week	3.58 lbs
1 month	14.5 lbs
6 months	5- to 20-lb tanks

Dual Mantel Propane Lamp 20 hrs/day

Period	Fuel Consumed
1 day	21.8 oz
1 week	10 lbs
1 month	2- to 20-lb tanks
6 months	8- to 20-lb tanks

2. Battery Lanterns   Battery-powered lanterns are very common and are good in emergencies. However, batteries are a lot more costly than fuels, so these lanterns wouldn't be efficient for extended power outages beyond two weeks.

Courtesy of the Coleman Company

Battery lanterns are beneficial if you have a lot of batteries stored or rechargeable batteries with a reliable means to recharge them. (*See "Battery Chargers" on page 114.*) After all, they are the cleanest of the lantern choices and safest.

There are also rechargeable lanterns that come with the rechargeable batteries encased within the unit itself like the Coleman Twin Tube Rechargeable Florescent. It comes with

Coleman Twin Tube Rechargeable Florescent Lantern

an adapter to recharge off either a regular outlet, battery inverter, or a car lighter adapter.

Courtesy of the Real Goods

Rechargeable (nicad) batteries

A Valuable Lesson on Batteries

There's more than meets the eye with the garden variety battery. A quick look at what is out there will help you know what you have if you have to yank those D cells out of the boom box and put them to some *real* work!

Known from coast to coast, AAAs, AAs, Cs, or Ds are what most people think of when they think of batteries. But to really know how you want to spend your money you should know the pros and cons of the different types of AAAs, AAs, Cs, or Ds are out there:

▸ **Standard Batteries**   These are usually hanging by the checkout stands. They're the least expensive kind of batteries. They have the shortest life, therefore their use is limited during extended power failures. (You get what you pay for, as they say.)

▸ **Alkaline**   For pure power, alkalines are king. They last the longest on one charge, and they put out the brightest light. (Standard and alkaline are 1.5 Volts whereas nicads are less with 1.2 Volts.)

▸ **Rechargeables (nicad)**   A wonderful not-so-new development in battery technology. Nicads can be charged over 1,000 times! They are not as bright as alkalines and don't last as long on one charge. Nicads are susceptible to the cold. To get the best service from nicads, drain the battery all the way down until they drop off, and then recharge.

Battery Storage

To guarantee the longest life for batteries, store them separately from the flashlight, tool or appliance that you use them in. Most battery manufacturers stamp batteries with an expiration date so pay attention to this when you make your battery purchases.

Battery Chargers

With your nicads in hand, you'll need a battery charger that holds all the different size batteries you need. There's a variety of them out there varying in size, quality, and price from about $14 to $55. With a regular plug-in type, you'll have to either have a generator or a battery inverter to be able to make use of it. The 12-Volt nicad Charger ($25) allows you to plug it into your car lighter to recharge. Some chargers claim that they will recharge even the "noncharge-ables" for up to twenty times (Check out the Innovations Battery Manager—$55 Available from Real Goods catalog.)

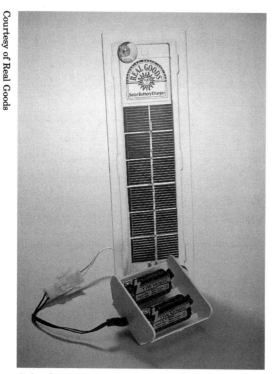

Courtesy of Real Goods

Solar battery charger

There are also solar rechargers that rely on the sun for power. There are several available through Real Goods or Jade Mountain. The Solar Super Charger ($30) will easily charge a couple of nicads in seven hours or less but it only holds two batteries at a time. Other solar chargers are available that charge more batteries at one time but they need to be left out in the sun for two days or more. Another way to take advantage of the sun's powers is to connect a basic solar panel directly to a rechargeable lantern or battery recharger.

Battery Lantern Running Times

The Coleman Company gives some tips on how to get the most life out your batteries along with some data of estimated use times from the tests that they have conducted. The evaluations are based on the Coleman Northstar Lantern and the Fluorescent Tube Rechargeable Battery Lantern. Keep in mind that there are many variables that effect efficiency, including brightness, duration of use, and temperature. But at least this gives you an idea of what to expect.

- Northstar battery electric lantern (Used with alkaline batteries)
    a) Has adjustable light so it can be more efficiently controlled. The lower the light, the longer the batteries will last.
    b) Estimated run time on high is up to eight hours and on low up to twenty hours.
    c) Comes with a night-light that will run up to 100 hours.
- Coleman Fluorescent Twin Tube Lantern
    a) Will give longer run times since you can use either one tube (eighteen hours on high) or two tubes (twenty-four hours on high).
    b) Intermittent use saves battery power.

3. Flashlights Flashlights are not designed to substitute for emergency lighting, that's what lanterns are for. Flashlights are more task oriented for things like walking, refueling gas tanks, making repairs, etc.

Things to remember about flashlights:

- Store several batteries for any long-term power outage problem, or
- Use rechargeable nicad batteries and battery charger.

- Rotate batteries at least every three months.
- Don't store batteries in the flashlight. However, keep them in close proximity so you can find the flashlight and the batteries in low-light or the dark if you would have to.

Flashlight "D" Cell Dry Batteries

Type of Use	Batt. Condition	Approx. Life
Continuous	new	5-6 hrs
	old	2-4 hrs
Intermittent	new	7-8 hrs
	old	3-5 hrs

4. Additional Backup Choices   In terms of endurance and output of light, the first three light sources discussed in this section—gas lanterns, battery lanterns, and flashlights—were presented in order of perceived value and usefulness, best to worst, although they certainly aren't the only alternate sources of light during extended blackouts. Some of the other limited options include:

a. Solar flashlights
b. Wind-up flashlights
c. Candles
d. Chemical light sticks

Courtesy of the Real Goods

Solar flashlight

a. Solar flashlights These are a great development and perfect for many emergency situations. Emergency experts have raved about the SolarVerter Flashlight. This is a neat unit where the body of the light is a small solar panel. If there's no sun, don't worry about it. Put in two AA batteries and you're off and running. With built-in solar batteries, it will go for about two-and-a-half hours, with alkaline batteries it will go triple that. The flashlight also functions as a solar battery charger for AA size batteries. (Available at Jade Mountain or Real Goods)

b. Wind-up flashlight   How about a wind-up flashlight for the ultimate in emergency preparedness? Made by the BayGen Company, you can wind this puppy up for about a minute to get about four to five minutes of run time. It will also run off nicad batteries or the twelve-volt adapter in the car. It costs around $75. This unit does not come with a radio.

Courtesy of the Real Goods

Wind-up flashlight

c. Candles   These are more of a last resort than good preparation. Unless they're enclosed in some kind of candle lantern, candles are a serious fire hazard, and they don't provide much light. An average candle will burn for about eight hours, and an oversized candle will burn for about forty-eight hours. However, you can get emergency slow burning candles. The Nuwick candles will burn for over one hundred hours. They come in a wide-based unbreakable metal tin, which makes them very stable.

Courtesy of the Real Goods

Nuwick candles

Tallow Candles Burning Rate

Height	Diameter	Approx. Life
6"	1/2"	3
6"	1"	8
9"	2"	48

d. Chemical light sticks   These are colorful tubes full of a chemical that glows when you bend the tube. They're perfect when you're outside refilling stove and lantern tanks since there is no flame. The sticks store for three years and give out eight to twelve hours of light. They don't store well in heat, so if you have them in the glove compartment of your car, rotate them every six

Courtesy of Major Surplus and Supply

Chemical light sticks

months. They come in several colors; the brightest colors to get are green and yellow.

Lighting mistakes:

- Thinking candles and flashlights are enough
- Not having enough fuel or batteries for your lanterns
- Not having the correct replaceable parts i.e., mantels, globes, etc.
- Buying a rechargeable lantern or batteries with no means of charging them

CHAPTER 4

HEALTH AND HYGIENE

"There is very little realization that there will be a disruption. As you start getting out into the population, I think most people are again assuming that things are going to operate the way they always have. That is not going to be the case."

—Sherry Burns, Director of Year 2000 Office
Central Intelligence Agency (CIA)

Surviving Y2K by stocking provisions—food, water, and electricity—should take care of our basic needs, but what about day-to-day concerns such as headaches, fevers, upset stomachs, toothaches, diarrhea, cuts or scratches, poison ivy or bug bites, sprained ankles, broken arms, or ear infections? The list goes on and on, and the severity of potential consequences climbs higher and higher. And these aren't even really serious medical problems. A medicine cabinet full of aspirin, Band-Aids, gauze pads, and ace bandages won't be enough. Let's take it a dreadful step further. A heart attack is serious business, but what if, on top of that, emergency response services are severely limited on or after January 1, 2000? A frightening thought is that the most dire of scenarios may be well within the realm of possibilities considering that the health care industry is one of the least prepared for disruptions from Y2K.

Studies in early 1999 showed that the health care industry has been given the worst grade (D-) for Y2K preparedness of all major industries. The U.S. Senate's Y2K report in March 1999 said, "sixty-four percent of hospitals say they don't plan to test their Y2K fixes to make sure they work." That means there may not be much help from nurses, physicians, dentists, oral surgeons, and hospitals for at least the first week or two of Y2K, if not longer. With serious Y2K problems, many of us are going to quickly find out just how much people depend on health-care professionals and facilities in times of need.

"The health care community is in serious trouble due to anticipated problems of the Y2K changeover," Joel Ackerman, executive director of the Minneapolis-based Rx2000 Solutions Institute, told the U.S. Senate Special Committee on the Year 2000. "Patient care and patient lives are at stake," Ackerman said. A recent survey revealed that 94 percent of health professionals questioned felt that "Y2K issues have significant potential to create errors that will lead to unnecessary deaths in health care."

In an industry riddled with the millennium bug—from 911 response capabilities, medical equipment failures, and electronic medical records to electronic exchange with insurers, manufacturing and/or distributing drugs, and more—failure is too horrible to contemplate. Consider the problems in a medical emergency in January 2000 if telephones, thus 9-1-1, aren't working. Remember, you need a new mindset to deal with this whole Y2K thing. Clearly in such a complex industry, where breakdowns are possible on so many fronts, it is crucial that people prepare to manage their own health and medical needs as best they can.

Learning Self-Reliance

If we don't trust that medical services will always be there, perhaps we'll take better care of ourselves. When preparing for any emergency, it's wise to be in the best possible physical shape. Everyone should have a pair of comfortable sturdy shoes to walk long distances if necessary. We may have to learn to do a lot more walking and physical work, like splitting and carrying wood, hand-washing clothes and many other things we now take for granted. Emergencies often demand more of us physically. This is important for yourself, but also keep in mind no one wants to become a burden to those around them.

Also, drink plenty of water! It's recommended that you drink two quarts per day for maximum health. Before you ever ration stored water, find another water supply and treat it. The bottom line of preparedness is keeping everyone healthy.

With all that in mind, let's dive into health care issues more deeply. Here are five areas that address being prepared for your health needs as well as those of your loved ones:

> **A. Advance Medical Planning**
> **B. Basic First Aid**
> **C. Vitamins and Herbs**
> **D. Personal and Family Hygiene**
> **E. Sanitation and Refuse**

A. Advance Medical Planning

Don't let the Year 2000 creep up on you without making some detailed medical preparations. It's often been said that if you don't have your health then nothing else matters. Adequate health and medical planning is crucial for dealing with Y2K. In this section there are five recommendations for advance Y2K crisis health plans.

➤ Have any dental and medical work done well before the end of 1999 and try not to schedule elective surgery just before or after the new year. With so many unknowns about the condition of the health care system and areas of possible failure—loss of medical records, confusion with health care insurance companies, shortages of pharmaceutical drugs, and more—getting any kind of medical or dental treatment could be difficult for some time after January 1, 2000. This assumes that your doctor is even available! The kind of severe medical emergency that Y2K may bring will require medical personnel to focus on only the most critical cases.

▶▶ Get prescription medicines filled before January 1. If possible, get enough refills to last a couple of months into the new year. Medications, for some, are a matter of life and death. Records could be lost so keep copies of your own prescriptions. Most pharmacies provide this information with medications. After Y2K, be prepared to bring cash to the pharmacy to purchase medications in case your health care insurance information is inaccessible.

If your doctor refuses to take your concerns about Y2K seriously, get another doctor. Getting medications in advance can be problematic in today's managed care environment, so work the system as best you can. Each case is different. What would they do if you were going on a three month vacation?

▶▶ If you wear glasses, make sure you have an extra pair. And while you're at it, you should have your eyes tested (especially if it has been at least three or four years since your last checkup) to see if your vision has changed. Granted, glasses aren't cheap, and you may have already spent a lot more than you wanted to on Y2K preparations, but this is a wise precautionary expense. Just as large hospitals may experience major problems so might your eye doctor.

▶▶ Take an advanced first-aid class, such as CPR. Learning how to handle emergencies will help reduce the stress in everyone around you, and could save a life. The better trained you are to handle medical emergencies, the better off you, and those around you, are if normal medical services are limited. Major cities and many smaller ones have

Red Cross offices that offer training programs. Call the Red Cross for locations and classes in your area.

▶ Have a good first-aid kit stocked and handy. During any kind of emergency, it is crucial that you have a well-supplied kit. Don't let your life or those of your loved ones hang in the balance in the hope that nothing will happen to anyone in your family during a Y2K medical crisis. No matter how much you know about first aid, without the proper equipment there's not much you can do. Learning as much as you can about advanced first aid is important, but the first step is having a good first-aid kit and any other medical equipment you may need.

Most sporting goods stores and survivalist retailers carry a wide assortment of first-aid kits, ranging from the basic glove compartment variety to kits that rival the family doctor's trusty black bag. Of course, the prices for these kits vary, too. A small basic kit from Wal-Mart will cost around $10. For a more comprehensive kit certified by the Emergency Medical Technicians (EMT) you will need to go to a medical supply store or camping store and may pay over $200. You can pick up a good mid-priced kit for anywhere between $40 and $80 that includes an assortment of first-aid supplies like bandages, wound dressings, moleskin, antiseptic swabs, gloves, and gauze tape. Of course, you can assemble your own supply kit, too. Using the First-aid Kit Checklist on page 177, take an inventory of what you already have, and buy what you are lacking. It is important to keep your supplies together in a box or bag in a designated place so everyone knows where to find it in an emergency. You can also order any of these supplies from Major Surplus and Supply at (800) 441-8855.

First-aid books are also valuable to have in emergencies. There are numerous first-aid books, like *First Aid and Emergency Procedures* ($29.95) from Family Physician's Home Emergency Company available in bookstores or at Amazon.com. This manual was originally written as a basic handbook for the U.S. Navy Hospital

Corps. It contains a lot of simple treatments for hundreds of conditions and is designed for independent care in the absence of a physician.

For the largest and most comprehensive collection of medical supplies and equipment there's a kit to handle everything from basic first aid to severe injuries—Hospital-in-a-Box. It is available from the Family Physician's Home Emergency Company. The kit comes with a video showing many advanced emergency procedures and twelve hundred supplies like splints, thermometer, anesthesia, the first-aid manual mentioned above, as well as more routine first-aid items like dressings, bandages, and ointments. It's pricey but for large families, neighborhoods, or community groups, the cost could be shared. Hospital-in-a-Box regularly costs $795. For a complete list of items included (or to order the kit or manual), contact Family Physician's Home Emergency Company at (877) FAM-PHYS (326-7497). (*See "Health" under Preparedness Suppliers on page 183 for the mailing address.*)

B. Basic First Aid

This section has excerpts of a few basic first-aid techniques from Family Physician's Home Emergency Company, offered with their permission for you to study and have on hand. However, this is in no way intended to replace a good first-aid book or course.

▸ **Abrasions**   With this type of injury, spray the abrasion with Dermaplast, an over-the-counter topical anesthetic. Wait five to ten minutes for the medicine to numb the area. If dirt or gravel is imbedded in the abrasion, this must be irrigated well and every piece of sand or other foreign material must be carefully removed. Once this is done, apply an appropriate ointment like first-aid cream, triple antibiotic ointment, or Silvadene cream to a nonstick pad and apply the medicated pad directly to the abrasion. Wrap the area with a light to minimal tension using a three-inch elastic bandage. Change the dressing daily.

When changing the nonstick pad, remove carefully. If it is stuck, soak the pad for five to ten minutes with hydrogen peroxide or saline to free the pad without causing pain. Keep the wound dressed until seepage has stopped. This will give the skin time to repair itself with the least amount of scarring.

‣ **Blisters** Avoid breakage of the blister to allow healing without scarring or infection. If the blister breaks, try to keep the skin intact and apply first-aid cream, triple antibiotic ointment, or Silvadene cream in much the same way as described above. If a blister forms on the heel or ankle, it may have tremendous pressure inside from the fluid. In this case, release the pressure by puncturing the blister in the side with a needle. make sure you cleanse the surface with alcohol or soap and water prior to puncturing the blister. Once the fluid pressure is released, the pain from the blister will subside. It is best to make every effort not to break the blister sac because exposure of the underlying skin to air will be painful, prolong healing, and leave it vulnerable to possible infection.

‣ **Bleeding** With a combination pad or gauze pad, apply pressure over the area of bleeding. Depending on the location, this will usually stop the bleeding right away. With direct pressure, venous bleeding will usually stop within five minutes. Once bleeding is stopped, consider the best method of wound closure: a Band-Aid or larger bandage. Arterial blood flow from a small- to medium-sized artery will be unpredictable and may require prolonged direct pressure or even surgery to stop the flow. Bleeding from a large artery will require quick surgical intervention to avoid bleeding to death.

‣ **Swelling** Whenever the ankle, knee, or other extremity is swollen due to a sprain, fracture, or dislocation, the part affected should be wrapped with a compression dressing. A cold pack should be applied for the first twenty-four to thirty-six hours, with the injured extremity elevated higher than the level of the heart and rested. Use the ice pack on the area for ten minutes on and two hours off for the first twenty-four hour period after the initial injury, or until swelling and pain have subsided. Stay off the extremity for at least five days, with no weight-bearing activity. Physical therapy and rehabilitation should begin as soon as they can be tolerated, focusing on flexibility.

More serious sprains, where a "pop" may be felt or heard at the time of the injury, have either partially or completely torn the joint capsule and should be treated as though they were fractured. For these serious sprains, you should be immobilized for a minimum of three weeks to allow the best chance to heal. As soon as you can, have the wound X-rayed to determine if there is a fracture. In cases where extensive bruising, deformity, and instability are present, as with all sprains, the only way to rule out a fracture is with an X-ray.

▸ **Compression Dressing** These are dressings that apply a lot of pressure, hence the name. As noted above, they are used with wounds that cause swelling. To apply a compression dressing, wrap the wound tightly (but not so tight as to cut off circulation) with an elastic bandage. Compression dressings are also used to stop bleeding prior to surgical intervention. For these wounds, combination pads, gauze pads, or nonadhesive pads are used with the elastic bandages.

▸ **Eye Injuries** Eye injuries may infrequently require a dressing such as an eye patch. Most mild eye injuries require only eye drops such as Cortisporin ophthalmic solution—two drops, three times daily for three to five days. More serious eye injuries, such as laceration or embedded foreign objects, require professional help. In the case of chemical burns, flush with copious amounts of water or saline eyewash. Mix a teaspoon of sodium bicarbonate with one quart of water or saline and flush the eye thoroughly. Use Cortisporin ophthalmic solution three times daily for three to five days. if alkali, such as sodium hydroxide (lye, bleach solutions, or caustic soda), gets in your eye, you should see a doctor immediately after flushing. It will dissolve tissues, such as eyeball, eyelids, or any other body part. This may permanently blind the eye even with the best medical help.

▸▸ **Poisoning** Use Syrup of Ipecac to induce vomiting—this is to be used in situations where the substance ingested is poisonous but will not increase harm by coming back up the esophagus a second time. Inducement of vomiting for substances such as gasoline or other petroleum distillates are not recommended because they may be inhaled (aspirated), thus causing a petroleum-induced pneumonia. Consult a poison control center for more complete information.

An Important Note About Medical Devices

Barb Cole-Gomolski, senior editor of *ComputerWorld*, reports, "Health-care providers are accusing medical device makers of leaving them in a potential lurch come Year 2000 by failing to give them sufficient warning that their equipment could fail to function." Numerous medical devices use embedded chips that are cyclically controlled and date sensitive including IV pumps, respirators, EKG equipment, and dialysis machines. Telemetry computers are another type of date-sensitive equipment used in operating rooms. They allow medical technicians to read pulse, blood pressure, temperature, EKG (the heartbeat), and scan the history of the patient. These pieces of equipment are very expensive to replace, but as one doctor told us, "If [hospitals] are looking to be open in 2000, they're going to have to fix [the equipment]."

If your life depends on it, it's not worth the risk to take your chances and hope for the best. If you or anyone you know is dependent on medical devices such as IV pumps or dialysis machines, contact the manufacturer and get their assurance in writing that the equipment is Y2K compliant. Be insistent and do your research. Unfortunately, there are no easy answers when it comes to this issue because a letter may be good to have for a lawsuit, but what do you do if the equipment fails to work? Some doctors have even received letters from their malpractice insurance carriers saying that if anything can be construed to be a Y2K-related incident, then they are not covered. Nonetheless, if a family member requires the use of a date-sensitive life-support system, FEMA (Federal Emergency Management Agency) warns that these individuals should register with their local Emergency Management Office—Y2K or not. If worse comes to worse, you must be prepared to go to a hospital or a capable emergency shelter with backup generators to be assured of the medical services you need.

A Note About Children

Make sure your children are immunized against measles, mumps, tetanus, hepatitis B, and chicken pox.

Baby Tip - A Quick and Handy Remedy for Colic

When a baby gets colicky, it's hard on the baby and you. Lil' Tum-eeze will work but it's expensive. For a quick and easy remedy crush up a Rolaids and add it to a couple of teaspoons of water. All it takes is a dropper full—about 1 teaspoon. As always, check with your pediatrician first.

A Note about Elderly People

Since most people over the age of sixty-five experience a drop in their ability to absorb B-vitamins in food, they need to pay special attention to their diets. Riboflavin (vitamin B2) is fundamental to basic life energy and keeping us healthy. It is crucial in the production of red blood cells and anti-bodies that fight illnesses. Foods with riboflavin include beef liver, chicken, milk products, kidney beans, and canned salmon. (The canned salmon and kidney beans are easy to include in any food storage plan.) To ensure the intake of B-vitamins, talk to your doctor about taking a supplement.

After age forty, the kidney function decreases by an average of 1 percent per year, causing a decline in the body's ability to be able to handle medications. Therefore, people over seventy years old should only take *half the normal adult dose* on almost all medications. You should take half doses of many over-the-counter medications, like Motrin, Aspirin, cough and cold medicines, and some antibiotics. Make sure you talk to your doctor about doses for prescription medication for things like high blood pressure and heart disease.

C. Vitamins and Herbs

For decades Americans have been programmed to think that the best available medical care comes in a pill prescribed by the doctor or bought over the counter. Aspirins make headaches go away; Alka-Seltzers or Tums cure nausea or heartburn; and Advil (Ibuprofen) will ease the pain of menstrual cramps. The problem in the United States is the attitude that good health comes from a pill instead of from a healthy diet. Ironically, this problem has been aggravated by the government agency—the FDA (Food and Drug Administration)—designed to protect us from such harms. For example, natural treatments for arthritis have been available in Europe and Asia for decades, but they have been made available in America only in the last couple of years with the publication of *The Arthritis Cure*. Much of the reason for this is that the major drug companies in America help fund the FDA through lobbying. These drug companies make the pharmaceuticals that are designed to relieve arthritis pain, so they have a vested interest in keeping arthritis around. Since the drug companies give money to the FDA, the FDA has a vested interest in keeping the drug companies happy. That is why doctors are encouraged to prescribe drugs rather than prescribe dietary or natural alternatives that may be more beneficial in the long run.

Good health is more about diet, exercise, vitamins, and herbs than about pills. Recently, these alternative healing therapies have begun to get the respect they deserve. It's surprising that the doctors dedicated to preserving life haven't been more curious about scoping out healing treatments that have been around for eons. The medical community may not be curious, but American consumers are. They're choosing health food stores over doctors' offices for their one-stop health care shopping. They're beginning to treat everything from colds and arthritis to fatigue and memory loss with natural supplements instead of drugs.

Given that Y2K preparedness is about self-sufficiency, you should use what's available to you. Make vitamins and herbs a part of your critical preparedness health kit. With Y2K, you might not have a choice about going to a doctor on short notice. There are numerous books on the subject of vitamins and herbs to expand your knowledge of their benefits. It is important to use these supplements in maintaining physical health and staying mentally clear and balanced during a time that could bring great stress. Let's take a quick look at the preventative measures of vitamins and the alternative medicine found in certain herbs.

Vitamins

In recent years, there has been a "vitamin revolution," as described by Jean Carper, author and leading authority on health and nutrition. "Fast disappearing is the dogma that food can give you everything you need to get through . . . This isn't the fault of nature for deliberately shortchanging us. Maybe (Mother Nature) didn't foresee the hazards modern civilization would bring," says Carper.

Vitamins have gained tremendous acceptance in our culture. Many of us are already used to taking multivitamins and other nutritional supplements with breakfast. Vitamins are particularly important for Y2K preparedness due to the fact that a limited food supply will mean fewer fresh fruits and vegetables. Since stored foods are often not as nutritionally rich as fresh foods, nutritional supplements may be our only source of vitamins. Also, stress is known to deplete the body of nutrients, and any emergency is prone to be stressful. For these reasons, it is important to store vitamin supplements.

Start out with a good multivitamin that contains vitamin A, B-complex, C, D, E, and a mix of minerals including Calcium, Copper, Chromium, Folic Acid, Iron, Magnesium, Potassium, Selenium, and Zinc. You can find these at the grocery or health-food store under numerous brand names. Take the vitamins with food for best results. A bottle will cost from $10 to $12 and usually contain 60 to 100 capsules. You should also have some big bottles of vitamin C and E for combating illnesses like the cold or flu. Here are some key vitamins that you should also include in a family vitamin health kit:

> ➤ **Vitamin C**   Research shows that people who take vitamin C regularly are healthier than people who don't. It is believed to help stave off colds and infections, and reduce the risks of cancer and heart disease. It also helps to heal wounds and lower blood pressure. Take at least 500 milligrams a day, optimally 250 milligrams twice per day. Buy big bottles of vitamin C, and don't forget to pass it around to everyone at the breakfast table!
>
> ➤ **Vitamin E**   As a powerful antioxidant, vitamin E inhibits

free-radicals, which are reactive atoms that cause degenerative diseases and cell death, including heart disease. (Some research indicates it may do wonders against Alzheimer's and prostate cancer.) In her book *Stop Aging Now!*, Jean Carper says that the two most important things you can take to slow aging are vitamin E and vitamin C. Take 400 IUs of vitamin E daily.

▸ **Calcium**   Take 1,000 to 1,200 milligrams of calcium a day in capsule form. It is particularly important for women in preventing osteoporosis, or bone loss. Many people assume they are getting enough from food—milk products, salmon, peanuts, potatoes, and kidney beans—but often aren't. To better absorb calcium, you need vitamin D, which primarily comes from sunlight. Older people in particular need to try to get enough sun in order to get enough vitamin D.

▸ **Omega-3 Fatty Acids**   The other name commonly used for omega-3 fatty acids is fish oil, which, not so coincidentally, is where you can get this powerful substance. Essential fatty acids are getting a whole new respect because of their many benefits, including lowering cholesterol, controlling blood pressure, treating some digestive problems, and preventing heart attacks. (Some research shows that it could even prevent cancer.) Canned salmon, sardines, and tuna will go a long way toward protecting your health in a food shortage. Besides fish, you can also get omega-3 fatty acids in olive oil, canola oil, corn oil, soybean oil, and safflower oil. You can get the same benefits from a daily supplement of 1,000 milligrams a day.

Herbs

Herbal medicines offer inexpensive remedies for many health conditions, and the more you know about them, the better you can put them to use. Following is a list of some common and useful medicinal herbs to include in your Y2K preparedness plans. These

herbs should not be used to replace medicines prescribed by your
doctor but supplement them. (This chart is not intended to be a di-
agnostic chart. Review books and literature that provide further
information and/or consult a qualified herbalist.)

Herbal Health Kit

Herbs	Take this for ...	Form
Aloe Vera	burns, wounds, and dry skin	Gel
Angelica (good all-around tonic)	poor circulation, irregular menstrual cycles, and congestion	Capsule Tincture Liniment
Arnica	bruises, aches, strains, swelling, and inflammation associated with arthritis, rheumatism and, phlebitis	Oil Liniment
Barberry	stimulating the immune system, and relieving symptoms of liver disease, hepatitis, jaundice, drug abuse, and alcoholism	Capsule Tincture
Bee Pollen	colds and allergies	Capsule
Black Cohosh (DO NOT USE DURING PREGNANCY. Best taken under observation of herbalist.)	menstrual cramps and muscle spasms; relief from nervous conditions like insomnia, neuralgia (like migraines), numbness, and convulsions	Capsule Tincture
Coenzyme Q-10 (strong antioxidant properties; NOT a substitute for prescribed heart medications)	strengthening the heart and high blood pressure	Capsule

Herbs	Take this for ...	Form
Comfrey (external use only)	treatment of wounds and sores and stopping bleeding.	Ointment Skin cream
Echinacea	stopping a cold, if taken early enough and helping stimulate immune system	Capsule Tincture Spray
Evening Primrose	reducing PMS symptoms, hypertension, relieving anxiety, arthritis	Gel cap
Feverfew	chronic headaches, constipation, menstrual cramps, and anxiety.	Capsule
Fish Oil or Omega-3	strengthening the heart, blood, joints, colon, and brain	Gel cap
Garlic (natural antibiotic, broad-based infection fighter, and overall tonic)	colds and digestion	Raw Tablet Oil
Ginko (antiaging tonic)	improving blood circulation, increasing memory	Capsule
Ginger	relieving nausea and indigestion, morning sickness, colds, bronchitis, and flus	Capsule Tincture Ginger Ale
Glucosamine	relieving osteoarthritis and rebuilding damaged cartilage.	Capsule
Goldenseal (natural antibiotic)	digestive problems such as colitis and gastritis and treating upper respiratory problems such as bronchitis and hay fever.	Capsule Tincture
Kava	relieving anxiety, muscle spasms, tension headaches, and mild insomnia	Capsule

Herbal Health Kit (*continued*)

Herbs	Take this for . . .	Form
Licorice	coughs, remedying cold and flu symptoms, and constipation	Capsule Tincture
Milk Thistle (liver tonic)	increasing the flow of milk for nursing mothers	Capsule
Saw Palmetto	prostate problems	
Siberian Ginseng	improving physical stamina and mental alertness, and relieves physical stress.	Capsule Tincture
Valerian	insomnia and relieving anxiety	Capsule Tincture Tablet

Like food, vitamins and herbs should be stored in a cool dry place to maximize their shelf life and maintain full potency. Most labels will give an expiration date, but in general, shelf life will extend up to three to five years. You don't have to worry about toxicity after expiration, just a loss of potency.

D. Personal and Family Hygiene

Visualize a mini-convenience store in your home. To have adequate supplies of everyday products stockpile toothpaste, mouthwash, deodorant, soap, aspirin, feminine supplies, towels, and other items your family uses regularly. Review the Personal and Family Hygiene Checklist at the back of the book for items to add to your shopping list. Here are key factors to consider:

> ‣ **Brushing Teeth** With possible Y2K water problems, it is important to make sure the water you use to brush your teeth is drinkable.
> ‣ **Washing Yourself** Approach washing and bathing as if

you were on a backpacking or camping trip by planning to take sponge baths with washcloths, stored water, and soap. If you have the fuel to spare, heat some water on the camping stove for a hot sponge bath. If you live in a warm climate, you can get a solar shower for about $15 at surplus supply and camping stores. A black bag absorbs the heat of the sun to heat the water. With a hose and nozzle attached on the bottom end, after you let the water heat up, hang it in your shower and have at it!

‣ **Washing Clothes** Be sure to wash all your clothes on or around December 31, 1999, so you don't go into January 2000 with a lot of dirty clothes. After that, without electricity, you'll have to wash your clothes by hand. Liquid detergent works well, but if necessary you can also use regular dish detergent. To dry clothes without a dryer, hang them outdoors, weather permitting, or near a heat source indoors.

‣ **Using the Toilet** Some preparedness experts avoid this topic and assume people will figure it out on their own. The first thing to do is fill all bathtubs, sinks and even garbage cans, with water on New Year's Eve so that in a water shortage, you'll have a good supply of "flushing" water. Flushing water is water that you can use to fill the tank on your toilet. The tank does not need to be completely full to flush, so you should experiment before hand to find out the minimum amount of water needed to flush the toilet. Water delivery most likely won't be a long-term problem, but if it is, sawdust and lye should be used to treat any outdoor waste disposal. Designate a place outside, preferable a hole, as the bathroom, and cover the waste with sawdust and/or lye to keep the smell and flies away.

E. Sanitation and Refuse

Plan for delays in garbage pickup by having a couple of extra garbage cans with tight lids that can hold refuse for at least two weeks. Separate your trash into burnable, food, and the rest. This will help keep the amount of garbage you produce to a minimum. You can burn all cardboard or paper products in the fireplace (in small amounts at a time), woodstove, or a designated place outside (check with local authorities to make sure outside burning is allowed). You can bury food waste outside in a mulch pile where it will decompose rapidly (it is good for the soil). Composted garbage includes orange and banana peels, lettuce ends, leftover macaroni and cheese—in other words, all of the organic stuff. To compost, you can purchase a ready-made composter, make one, or simply dig a hole in the backyard and layer the leftovers with dirt. Turn the garbage every week or so with a shovel or pitch fork to aerate and help it decompose. This will smell nasty, so keep putting dirt on it. There are ready-made boxes that have air holes in them so you don't have to do this. With those, you put the garbage in the top and as things sift down, you can open a little door at the bottom and out comes excellent natural fertilizer!

Practicing good sanitation is vital for keeping everyone healthy in an emergency. Scraps of food and crumbs are a magnet for insects and bacteria. To prevent illness, stock up on plenty of cleaning supplies: sponges, mops, buckets, and good antibacterial cleaning solutions. A clean living area also helps to keep morale up among the family. Just because you may be living with inconveniences in an emergency situation doesn't mean that you let everything go to pot. (*See Sanitation and Refuse Checklist on page 178.*) Here are some important cleaning reminders:

- Keep counters and cooking surfaces clean by wiping them down with antibacterial soap after every meal. Use disinfectant regularly.

- Thoroughly wash your hands before every meal.
- Separate your trash, burying your food trash to keep bugs outside.
- Use bug killers where necessary to control insects.

CHAPTER 5

MONEY

What a rude awakening it would be to go to your bank the first week of January 2000 and find that they have no record of your most recent deposit. Or, maybe you'll receive an ominously worded notice from your mortgage company informing you that they have no record of your latest payment. Maybe you will get a bill from your insurance company for unpaid premiums dating back a hundred years. Then, to add to your troubles, what if the stock market nosedives by 25 percent in a week with no sign of an upswing.

There is good news: Reports indicate that the banking and financial services industry is among the most prepared in the United States to make a relatively smooth transition into the next century. Smaller banks and credit unions are more at risk because of a lack of resources. In other words, it appears less likely that banks will lose their customers' records. That's not to say that there will be no problems, so keep good records. However, a bank's Y2K readiness doesn't protect it from loan defaults if their customers aren't compliant and can't pay their loans or mortgages. It's this kind of Y2K problem that will have the longest lasting impact on the banking industry. According to a recent study by

Gartner Group, an international consulting firm specializing in Y2K problem remediation, 15 percent of U.S. companies will experience a mission-critical failure. Michael Curtiss, Y2K consultant to the Federal Reserve, the U.S. Treasury, and a number of banks, estimates that large banks will not fail, but that 1,500 smaller and mid-sized banks could experience vendor software difficulties for one to ten days. He says that three hundred of these could have problems lasting longer than thirty days and will probably not stay in business. You should ask for a written statement from you bank telling you they are compliant. If they cannot send you a statement of compliance, it is likely that they aren't and won't be by the Year 2000.

Safety Ratings for Your Bank

Contact a financial research company to determine the financial safety rating of your bank.

Veribanc   (800) 442-2657
    $10 for the first bank
    $5 for each additional bank

Weiss Research   (800) 291-8545
    $15 for verbal rating per bank
    $40 for quarterly updates in writing

As for the economic system itself, the strength of the U.S. government will get us through the Y2K crisis without total economic collapse, but that doesn't mean that the stock market won't get slammed. For that reason, Y2K-knowledgeable financial advisers recommend to protect your financial assets and offer some thoughts on how to profit in a Y2K recession.

Some of the ways to protect your investments is by keeping good records, which translates to paperwork, which in turn translates to headaches or nightmares for most people. Even in this computer age, life can be a never-ending paperwork headache. Look at Y2K preparedness as an opportunity to organize your financial life. Keeping track of money, assets, and documentation begins with organization and prioritizing, and no one knows best how to handle your unique needs better than you do. To deal with your family's records and financial assets, look at the following four broad areas in the rest of this chapter:

> **A. Documentation**
> **B. Money and the Post-Y2K Economy**
> **C. The Stock Market**
> **D. General Financial Preparedness**

A. Documentation

Since most records are kept on computers, it is important to assemble hard copies of all important personal, business, and family documents. If the Y2K crisis causes computers to erase records or temporarily freezes access to them, it is important to be able to prove who you are, what accounts you have, and their standing. Everything should be as current as possible. Sure, preparing for the holidays can be a distraction, but don't let it be this year! Stay on top of your paperwork. It is important to keep bank statements, deposit slips, credit card statements, and proof of payment of insurance premiums in case of miscalculations and erroneous reports.

Family Documents to be Safely Secured and Stored

Keep these records in a container that is accessible, portable, secure, and fire-resistant.

- Wills, insurance policies, contracts, deeds, stocks, and bonds
- Medical records, prescription records, and dental records
- Passports, social security cards, and immunization records
- Current bank account statements, and canceled checks (to show proof of payment)
- Credit card account statements
- Family records (birth, marriage, and death certificates)
- Inventory of valuable household goods, important telephone numbers

You should store all these documents in a fireproof safe. There are all kinds of safes available. The more expensive kinds mount in a wall or floor and cost from $300 to $800. Otherwise, you can get a portable fireproof safe from Wal-Mart or Kmart for $80 to $150. If you get a portable safe, or decide to hide your valuables, pick a good hiding place and be sure to tell another trusted family member the location. Don't laugh; it's easy to forget where you have hidden things. For added protection, make backup copies of documents and store them in a second secure spot.

Safety Deposit Box

If you have valuables or documents stored in a bank safety deposit box that you think you may need in the first two weeks of January 2000, consider removing them during December 1999, just in case.

If you have valuables in a safety deposit box, make sure there's nothing in it that you will need in the first week or two of January 2000. Banks will be dealing with whatever glitches happen. In the confusion of coping with lost or erroneous records and defaulting loans, banks may not have time to open their vaults.

B. Money and the Post-Y2K Economy

"Any company that neglects this looming problem is simply asking for trouble. If a firm is eventually hit by a Year 2000 breakdown, it will probably be put out of business—not by the authority of any regulator, but by the power of the market itself. And its not just the institutions I'm concerned about. Its the investors who do business with them. A Year 2000 breakdown could do incalculable damage to investors' finances, and could undermine their confidence in our entire financial structure."

—Arthur Levitt Jr.,
Chairman, Securities and Exchange Commission

"Some people with technological expertise think the whole 'millennium bug' issue is overblown. Don't you believe it. Comments that doubt the seriousness of the problem are dead wrong."

—Edward Kelly, Federal Reserve Board
The Miami Herald, March 1, 1998

Some people suggest the pending Y2K crisis will cause a run on banks as people make sure their money is safe—in their hands—leaving the economy in rubble while we try and pick up the pieces in a postapocalyptic world. It looks like no industry will go unscathed, but take comfort in knowing that of any industry in the U.S., the banking industry gets the highest grade for Y2K readiness due in large part to federal regulators enforcing early and aggressive testing programs.

For those of you comparing Y2K to the Great Depression, one major difference is that the Fed (Federal Reserve Board) and the FDIC (Federal Deposit Insurance Company) simply didn't exist following the stock market crash of 1929 or into the 1930s. The Fed and the FDIC will aid banks in trouble. They did it in the savings and loan scandals of the 1980s, and they'll do it for the Y2K crisis, too. John Mauldin, author of *How to Profit in a Y2K Recession*, also shares this confidence in the U.S. Treasury.

"Consider this: In the last century, this country was torn in two by civil war. In 1941, Japan's war planes bombed Pearl Harbor and German U-boats circled our shores. In 1980, our markets were thrown into turmoil by rip-roaring inflation. Just two years ago, the federal government was forced to shut down because of the budget battle. But even during all those emergencies, the U.S. Treasury never missed a payment—even by one day."

The economic system as a whole should survive, however, that's not to say that Y2K won't deliver a significant wallop to the economy that will likely affect us all.

Greenbacks to Go

The Federal Reserve is well aware that some people will want to stockpile some cash just in case. So to handle the demand, they are printing an extra $50 billion in mixed denominations. This is not an inflationary move on the part of the Fed because the cash is actually being traded with your checking or savings account money. The overall money supply is not actually increased.

The Y2K Wallop

Any economic system based on paper currency relies on the people's confidence in the promise that the paper is worth something. It is this confidence that could determine the wallop that Y2K could deliver following infrastructure breakdowns, like food, water, and electricity availability. The more confident the people are that the government will fix everything the more likely they are to keep their money in the system: banks, stocks, bonds, or the like. However, if people lose confidence in the government during the Y2K crisis, there may be a run on the banks and a drain on the economy. Regardless of the confidence of the people, banks will certainly be hit hard if any of the major utility or telecommunications services fail. FDIC Chairman Donna Tanoue noted at a meeting of the President's Council on Year 2000 Conversion that "banks, insurance companies and brokerage houses can be ready for the century date change but will find it difficult to continue operations without infrastructure services such as telecommunications and energy. It has been difficult to assess the state of Year 2000 readiness in these areas."

Even if the entire banking industry, telecommunications industry, and all utility companies were 100 percent compliant, there is still a threat to banks since 15 percent of U.S. companies will experience mission-critical failures. It is likely mission-critical failures will cause disruptions major enough to lead to bankruptcies and closures. If that happens, there will be a lot of defaulted loans that could jeopardize banks. When referring to Y2K, Alan Greenspan, Chairman of the Federal Reserve said, "Inevitable difficulties are going to emerge. You could end up with . . . a very large problem."

I am not a financial expert and am merely presenting thoughts and opinions of far more knowledgeable people. Ed Yardeni, Chief Economist of Deutsche Bank Securities and international economic adviser on Y2K, has projected a 70 percent chance of a global recession due to Y2K business chaos around the globe.

Experts predict that Y2K-related economic disruptions will cause a recession at least as severe as the oil embargoes of 1973-74, which caused the Dow Jones Average to drop 43 percent from its high. At that time, energy was the critical resource needed to run industry; today it is the flow of information that drives the core of our economy. Americans are linked by the massive flow of information and are not insulated from the economic fates of those around the world.

Yardeni suggests that this recession could begin during the second half of 1999 as the public takes precautions against future uncertainties by holding off on large purchases. Will Hepburn, a Y2K savvy financial adviser in Prescott, Arizona, believes that "even if the technical problems of Y2K are taken care of, the sheer uncertainty of what could happen will cause people to change their spending patterns. As the specter of Y2K grows, all of a sudden people will begin to hold back on spending on big ticket items like cars, houses, etc." He explains how this uncertainty will affect the economy by saying, "This type of spending directly reflects a consumer's confidence in the future. The approach of Y2K will steadily erode consumer confidence causing more and more purchases to be put off. It doesn't take a large portion of the population to react fearfully to affect the overall economy because of the size of these expenditures. Their absence can and (fairly quickly) will cause a widespread economic downturn, or *deflation*."

Ironically, the most serious risks that businesses face from Y2K emanate more from outside forces than internal ones. Of course, those businesses that ignore the Y2K problem altogether or have no resources to correct it could well become its victims. As for the large companies, they have the budgets and staff to deal with Y2K remediation, but they could see the biggest brunt come from less prepared suppliers and breakdowns in overseas business dealings as international companies flounder in their own Y2K messes.

The FDIC and Your Money

It's important to keep your deposit accounts within the federal insurance limits of $100,000. The accounts must be set up correctly. If you want more information or if you have questions about FDIC deposit insurance coverage, go to their Web site at www.fdic.gov, or talk to an FDIC insurance specialist or your banker.

C. The Stock Market

The stock market is the leading indicator of economic health. Since the summer of 1998, the market has been on the rise due in large part to the seductive headlines of a few growing stocks and the increase in day trading online. After all, the single most important driver of the economy and stock market is consumer confidence, which is measured by spending, and spending has been going on. However, as people get increasingly concerned about Y2K, the economy will soften. This doesn't mean that people don't have the dollars, but they may withhold spending and wait for prices to drop even further. The media seems to be ignoring the signs of this deflationary trend. (Certain parallels can be made between the last couple of years and the 1920s when Americans thought that good times would last forever with their newly electrified homes and inexpensive goods from new factories with assembly lines. Life was good and no one foresaw an end to the prosperity.)

As the saying goes, "The bigger they are, the harder they fall," and the stock market is as overvalued as it has ever been in history. The increase of investing in mutual funds, corporate pension plans, and bank-run index funds has helped to fuel the massive rise in the stock market. These funds and plans blindly follow the stock market and have no fund managers, which make them the cheapest investment funds to operate. Everyone loves a bargain but few realize that this means no one is at the controls to say, "Buying this stock at these prices is crazy." Therefore, the market continues to climb higher and higher like it was on autopilot.

Let's look at some important things to note about the stock market today: In 1998 the average stock on the New York Stock Exchange (NYSE) lost 4 percent of its value, but the public saw a stock market on the rise. That is because the the NYSE is one of several indexes that measures the stock market as a whole. In other words, because the top twenty-five companies out of this index showed an increase, the whole market showed an increase even though most of the companies may lose points. The same thing happens with the S&P Index and the Dow Jones Industrial Average. When a handfull of large companies show an increase, the index will show an increase even though the majority of the stocks are down.

When the markets begin experiencing losses suffered by the impact of the Y2K problem and the deflationary cycle, money will begin to flow out of the stock market and the Indexes will start to stumble. People will begin to realize this faltering and selling may increase, creating a downward spiral in stock prices just as blind and senseless as the recent upward spiral. "I expect that stock prices could fall at least 30 percent," says Yardeni, "I am not sure (exactly) when investors will start to discount Y2K in stock prices, but it will be by the summer of 1999." Financial adviser Will Hepburn adds, "No one knows exactly how Y2K will shake out, but I think it's fair to assume that Y2K will be in the top ten economic events of this century, if not number one, when history is finally written."

Safest Harbors for Your Money

Y2K-aware financial advisers are consistent in their recommendations to invest in Treasury bonds and notes. "Government bonds are a good safe harbor because they have never missed a payment and probably never will because the government has those printing presses," says Hepburn, "Also, the bond market is much bigger than the stock market with nine times the amount of money changing hands every day in bonds over stocks. This larger pool of buyers gives you more assurance that you can sell your bonds at a fair price anytime you want. This is called liquidity. In a deflationary environment, buyers hold onto their cash, and the ability to liquidate and convert assets to cash becomes even more valuable, making them far more liquid. The worse thing is you'd have to wait till (the bond) matures to redeem it at that point."

The bond markets are like a big teeter-totter with interest rates on one end and market values on the other. As interest rates go down, the value of bonds go up. In light of the unfolding recession, interest rates will likely drift downward, pushing bond prices up. During this period, which could extend into the Year 2000, long-term bonds will give the best returns. As interest rates begin to bottom out, a smart investor will begin to shift to short-term bonds for added stability and added liquidity.

Randy Flink, president of Championship Financial Advisers, echoes the same assertion toward bonds as he alludes to the impracticalities of total cash liquidity for realistic Y2K financial planning: "The decision to avoid Treasuries is in effect a decision to convert all financial instruments to tangible assets and banknotes. This task can be physically overwhelming if not logistically impossible for many people. (How much gold, silver and platinum bouillon can the average person conveniently transport and safely store?) I have to believe that in a state of economic crisis, the U.S. Government will prioritize the development and implementation of work-arounds for the U.S. Treasury and the Internal Revenue Service in order to protect its access to revenue."

Investing for Profit in a Y2K Economy

The importance of being liquid (being able to buy things) is often overlooked by investors. There will be some tremendous "bargain hunting" if the stock market drops because of Y2K. Good companies with great long-term prospects will be as undervalued after Y2K as they are overvalued today. And the markets never go in a straight line; they zigzag. There will be some powerful rallies even as the markets head downward. Investors who are nimble will have an opportunity to make a lot of money by investing during these rallies and sitting out the declines. Another strategy is to invest in a way that will make money if the market goes down. There is potentially as much money to be made in a declining market as a rising market.

You don't have to be a big-time Wall Street trader to play it smart. The old adage, "sell high, buy low" applies to a Y2K economy as well. If you sell your stocks and buy bonds now, you will benefit by selling high and buying low. After Y2K hits, you can sell the bonds high and get back into the stock market at reduced prices. It's the classic dream of investors—getting in and out of the markets at the right time. If you do nothing, your only option may be to sell low in the year 2000 and suffer losses.

One bit of advice is, *don't wait*. Since Y2K is such a well-known factor, many investors are saying to themselves, "If things start to look bad, I'll get out." The problem is analogous to being in a crowded rowboat where everyone shifts to one side at the same time. The imbalance will flip the boat. Investors who wait until deterioration becomes obvious to exit the markets could get crushed in the rush. It is better to be out of the market months early than one day late. The stock market dropped 23 percent in one day in 1987. The reason for this was simply supply and demand. There was an imbalance of buyers and sellers that day, a big imbalance, with many more sellers than buyers.

Unfortunately many investors have gotten lazy during the long bull market and have begun to believe Wall Street's siren song about buying and holding as the only way to invest. Investors who try to hold on to their favorites during Y2K may wait a long time to see their portfolios get back to 1999 levels. Investors in 1929 had to wait twenty years to see their portfolios break even.

Liquidity and flexibility will be the keys to financial success during the next few years. While the indexes languished in the 1970s, actively managed investments flourished. Market timing has gotten a lot of bad press from the Wall Street propaganda machines recently, because Wall Street wants everyone to stay invested. But this is just "spin," as slick and well financed as anything coming out of Washington. If you see a freight train coming, it makes sense to retain the ability to step off the tracks while it goes by. Market timing gives you this ability. Legendary investor Sir John Templeton says that investment styles cycle in and out of favor, sometimes for long periods of time. If you are locked in to a particular style of investing because it worked well in the long bull market of the 1990s, such as index fund investing, be aware that Y2K is changing the investment paradigm that made index investing so attractive. Since debt is a curse in a deflationary environment, real estate, too, could become a great bargain as properties burdened with large mortgages are foreclosed on and resold. This could be the opportunity of a lifetime to buy low-priced assets, perhaps leveraged with low-interest loans.

But it will take money to do it. Cash money. So holding assets that can be converted easily to cash is critical to a successful Y2K investment strategy. One thing that has changed about investing in the Y2K environment is the primary risk factors. A few years back, during the longest bull market in history, the biggest risk was getting left behind. A 13 percent market drop in 1997 signaled a change. The predominant risk became market risk with large, sudden swings in market prices. As we go through the threshold of the Year 2000, the predominant risk will become default risk companies who misjudge the Y2K factor and are crippled or bankrupted. The stocks and bonds of these companies will plummet in value. Shortly after Y2K, the primary risk will shift to inflation, meaning things denominated in dollars will become worth less than before. To successfully ride these investment cycles will take cash and a willingness to move it several times in several years.

Plan ahead for Y2K with your investments like you would with food or energy sources. Consult your financial adviser about your Y2K concerns and making adjustments to compensate for the new and unusual risks associated with Y2K. If your adviser is not sensitive to your concerns about Y2K, or is in denial about the problem, you have two choices: educate your broker about Y2K or find one who shares your views. It takes a strong ego to be an investment broker. Because of this, many brokers have a hard time backing away from earlier recommendations, even if they are no longer appropriate. Recognizing this factor can save you a lot of money at times like this.

D. General Financial Preparedness

Regardless of what you decide to do with investments and other very personal choices about your money, there are some basic ways to prepare. Because of probable power outages and, of course, computer failures, ATMs may be down for a few days. Therefore, you should have at least $500 on hand, or more if you can budget for it. Some experts even suggest having up to two to three months of living expense in cash, but that would be difficult for most families to do. To manage this, you need to sacrifice by spending less on "extras" and starting to stock some cash now in the same way you should buy extra food every time you go to the grocery store. If you're well prepared for Y2K overall, it should significantly reduce the amount of cash you need on hand. However, if you have not fully prepared, food and supplies could be expensive, requiring more cash to make necessary purchases.

A Word About Debt

With all the doubts about billing and payment information systems after January 1, 2000, it makes sense to reduce debt as much
as possible in 1999. That way you can steer clear of as many computer foul-ups as you can. Many businesses face difficulties—
insurance companies, colleges and universities (student loans),
phone companies, and utilities. If you can't get completely out of
debt this year, consider consolidating your bills in one low-interest
loan. Fortunately, credit card companies were hit with Y2K problems early due to Year 2000 expiration dates on cards. Entire
stores instantly shut down when error codes caused cash registers
to crash. (After this happened to Toys 'R Us, they quickly stepped
up their Y2K fix operation.) Events like these pushed credit card
companies into high gear on Y2K remediation programs, but that
doesn't mean there won't be further problems.

A Word About Gold

With Y2K brewing, there are many people who say gold coins or
bullion is the way to go. If you choose to buy gold to sleep well at
night, buy it. But, it should be viewed as a security blanket or insurance against total economic collapse, not as an investment.

In terms of day-to-day transactions, it's hard to trade a gold
coin for milk and bread. Unless the economy goes completely
belly-up and we're back to a trade/barter system (which is doubt-
ful), cash will still be preferred. However, if you think we may return to a trade/barter system, you may want to consider including
some junk silver coins in your mix of cash. These can be bought at
your local coin dealer.

In part, the frenzy to buy gold is being driven by people who
remember the last big recession in the 1970s where the price of
gold shot up to over $800 an ounce. However, the last time we had
a major *deflation* was in the 1930s when the price of gold dropped
like a rock to $30 an ounce. It's important to understand here that

in a deflation, the price of tangible assets tend to go down. Gold could well drop to $200 an ounce by the middle of 2000. The reason for this is that when everyone who bought gold pre-2000 because of Y2K fears realize they don't need it, the market will be flooded with sellers that will drastically drop gold prices.

Y2K Financial Preparedness Summary:

- Have at least $500 cash on hand.
- Pay bills ahead of time and keep canceled checks.
- Get out of debt as much as possible.
- Keep copies of all financial records (bank records, credit card invoices, phone and utility bills, etc. See complete "Financial/Personal Documents" Checklist).
- Get a copy of your credit report just prior to and just after January 1, 2000.
- If you are in the job market, get college transcripts.

CHAPTER 6

GENERAL FAMILY PREPAREDNESS

What will Y2K really mean for you and your family? Remember, the first few days, weeks, or even months of the Year 2000 will involve many changes and unfamiliar scenarios. When the smoke clears inside your head, you will find that the impact of Y2K extends far beyond food, water, electricity, health care and hygiene, and protecting your assets and documents.

This last chapter deals with aspects of life that will require some adjustments in attitudes and expectations. If you think you're going to escape from Y2K problems by hopping into your car and heading to the nearest sports bar, mall, or movie theater, think again. Chances are many of these places will be closed for at least the short term, so you're going to be stuck at home facing reality, working your way through a maze of Y2K challenges. That's what it is—a challenge you can overcome with planning and flexibility.

In closing the loop of your Y2K preparations, this chapter will summarize the following seven areas—some basics that will help you gear up for a return to simpler times (don't worry, you'll get over it):

    A. **Transportation**
    B. **Communications**
    C. **Security**
    D. **Tools and Repair**
    E. **Family Entertainment**
    F. **Moving**
    G. **Working through the Kinks**
    H. **Talking to Your Children about Y2K**

A. Transportation

> *"Reports used by the planners at FEMA indicate that the train system will be shut down by the Y2K bug, and power plants will not be able to stockpile enough coal to keep going while the problem is fixed."*

—An officer from the National Guard Bureau in Washington anonymously told *WorldNetDaily* in an exclusive interview

Think about waking up on January 1, 2000, walking out to your car for a trip to the grocery store to pick up some juice and eggs, and finding that your car won't start. Contrary to apocalyptic rumors, experts reassure us that car problems won't result from computer chip troubles. Embedded chips in cars are not date sensitive, so they don't care whether it's 1900 or 2000. Don't be lulled into complacency, however. Cars still require gas, and some gas stations will experience power failures. No electricity, no gas. Since it's not safe to store gas, make sure your tank is full on New Year's Eve.

As for airline travel, you should avoid being in flight at midnight 1999. The Federal Aviation Administration (FAA) has had enormous challenges in their Y2K remediation program. Many of air traffic control mainframe systems are more than twenty-five years old, and the original source code materials don't even exist anymore. If necessary, air traffic controllers could switch to manual systems and do what's called "flight rationing," or reduce the number of flights allowed to fly. That would mean, at best, chaotic and frustrating travel conditions. If you do fly, expect many delays and flight cancellations due to Y2K glitches.

International flights are expected to be particularly difficult in countries where Y2K has been largely ignored. (Canada, Great Britain, Sweden, Denmark, Norway, and the United States have made the most progress for Y2K remediation. Russia, Japan, and most East Asian, African, and Latin American nations are far behind.) Some airlines, such as Air France, have announced they will not fly after December 31, 1999, unless they are *completely* confident that every aspect of flight control, monitoring, and communication systems will function correctly. Recently, friends of ours tried to book a trip to London for the 1999 Christmas/New Year's holiday, but the airline said they weren't booking anything after December 1999 until further notice. So if you do go away over the holiday, be prepared to stay a while. *You have been warned.*

The railroad industry frequently has severe software malfunctions not related to Y2K, so don't assume that trains will be any more reliable than any other public transportation.

Have Wheels, Will Travel

Can you guess what the most efficient form of transportation will be, at least in the early stages of Y2K? That's right: the bicycle. For two to three hundred dollars, you can get a top-notch ten-speed or mountain bike. Check the classifieds for some great deals on used bikes.

Another way to go, so to speak, is with motorcycles. True, they require gasoline, but not much. Safety is always a concern, so use them at your own risk. And please, wear a helmet.

B. Communications

In the event of a power outage, you will need a working radio to find out what is going on. To plan ahead, store some nine volt batteries to run your clock radio. A Walkman could also fill the need, but then only one person can hear the news.

One alternative to battery-powered radios is windup/solar-powered models. BayGen and Dynamo are two companies that manufacture quality windup/solar-powered combination radio/flashlight units that have been used for years in third world countries. With a quick wind up, they'll run for up to half an hour. Otherwise, the solar panel can charge the units during the day. If you have some access to power, they come with an AC/DC converter. All the preparedness suppliers and many emergency food reserve companies carry one or both of these radios.

Major Surplus and Supply carries an exclusive line of BayGen AM/FM shortwave radios ($180) that come with an extension LED light. The light is connected to the radio with a twelve-foot cord so that you can place the light away from the radio for maximum convenience. These radios are so durable that they could be running 100 years from now.

As it has gained power, the Internet has become a primary means of accessing information for many of us. The Internet was originally conceived as a communications system designed to function in even the most serious of disasters, and Y2K should be no exception. Keep in mind that a typical laptop computer is going to get you a lot further since it requires very little power to operate compared to a desktop computer (Laptop, 20-50 watts; Desktop, 120 Watts). To power your laptop, a small battery and inverter for sensitive electronics will work fine. A small solar panel system designed to support laptops is another alternative.

If telephones aren't working, walkie-talkies and CB and ham radios will be effective for communication. They can be adapted to twelve-volt DC battery power for maximum efficiency.

C. Security

Home or office security won't be top priority for law enforcement officials if your area loses power and/or emergency services. Many people have also raised concerns that civil unrest and rioting could erupt, particularly in large urban areas, as anger and frustration build if Y2K problems delay entitlement checks like welfare, social security, disability, and others.

It was reported by *WorldNetDaily* that "The National Guard believes the nation's power grid will collapse and is making plans accordingly, according to the sources. Panic and widespread unrest are expected. Plans now call for a recall of all guard members placing an average of four thousand soldiers in each of the 120 largest cities." They went on to say that "The National Guard is planning . . . an exercise to practice a full mobilization of all 480,000 members of the National Guard . . . The exercise is planned to prepare for a possible mobilization in the event computer failures from the Y2K bug cause major disruptions of power, telecommunications, transportation, and banking."

It is not hard to imagine that emotions could run very high if there are power outages, phone failures, water deficiencies, and money shortages. People do desperate things in desperate times. If faced with these kinds of scenarios, the police and the National Guard will have their hands full.

Naturally, if power is interrupted, home security systems won't operate, so you can't count on this kind of warning system. Some security systems are designed to send an automatic signal to the police or a security monitoring station, but if telephones aren't working, these signals won't transmit. Even if the police were signaled of a break-in, most likely, they will be occupied with more serious emergencies.

Some people are planning on using a gun as their home security. Do *not* buy a gun if you have little or no prior experience with firearms. The idea is to steer clear of the battlefield, not join in the warfare. It takes hours of training to learn how to use a gun correctly. Dogs, on the other hand, are wonderful companions and can provide you with excellent security. Dogs have provided protection to their owners for eons. Most of us don't think of dogs in a utilitarian way, but it is a valuable service they can offer, with proper training. This is not something you do in November 1999. It takes time to work with a dog. The key is to establish a relationship of trust with your dog. When they bond with you and your family, their desire to protect is instinctive.

The best security for your family and property is a good neighborhood watch plan. Get to know your neighbors and share with them what you know about Y2K. The better prepared your neighborhood is, the safer you'll be.

Solar-powered outdoor lighting systems are a great way to help protect your property. You just stick them in the ground like garden stakes, and you're good to go. They work well and are reasonably priced at $75 to $100 apiece. (Check out Jade Mountain's wide variety of outdoor solar lights.) The beauty of outdoor solar light fixtures is that after they've been charging all day in the sun, you can also bring them indoors, if necessary, for additional lighting.

Prime Coach Outdoor Solar Light—S-2

If you are concerned about your valuables, a hidden home vault or safe offers good protection. Bank vaults are another safe alternative if you don't need access immediately. Some Y2K experts believe that banks will suffer more from building and security problems than actually losing account records. Because many bank security systems are controlled by computers, vaults could be inaccessible. Working through these problems could take time, so if you have things in a safety deposit box that you may need immediately after January 1, take them out before New Year's Eve.

D. Tools and Repair

When preparing your tool kit, make sure you choose hand-powered tools that don't need electricity to operate. Be sure to include tools for turning off water and gas and making repairs yourself. Things like hammers, screwdrivers, pliers, saws, utility knives, and wire cutters are essential preparedness items. (*See Tool Checklist on page 179.*)

Cordless drills are great, too, but get extra batteries that are fully charged before the new year. (With a battery inverter or generator, batteries can be recharged.)

Along with tools, it is important to have some supplies on hand. Be sure to have some nails, rope, duct tape, glue, caulk, screws, and plywood. Although you can't foresee everything, it is a good idea to be as prepared as possible.

If you can have a garden, make sure you have all the basic gardening tools on hand, like trowels, a rake, cultivator, and hoes. You and your neighbors may also want to share a hand-powered lawn mower.

E. Family Entertainment

Without electricity, America's favorite pastime, watching television, will come to an end. If you do have a means to power one with a generator, solar panel or battery inverter, a small TV will provide you with much longer service since it requires relatively little wattage to operate. Large TVs use a lot of electricity and therefore would use a lot of fuel to operate, fuel that could be used for cooking and heating. Without electricity, however, broadcasters may not be airing too much entertainment programming.

Save your sanity and plan for things children can do without electricity. Board games and puzzles can provide hours of fun for the whole family. Cards have long been an immediate and portable way to bring everyone together for a game of gin rummy, poker, hearts, old maid, or go fish. Stock up on your favorites and make the loser chop wood! (Although some might say the job should go to the winner.) Have lots of art supplies on hand: paper, crayons, paints, scissors, glue, and clay. All these things provide endless entertainment and could inspire the budding artist in your child and maybe you, too!

Without TV, you might finally get to those books you've been telling yourself for years you would read. Of course this may be a great opportunity to encourage the kids to read, too, so have lots of books on hand. In this electronic age of video games, Nintendo, movies, and computers, many of us have lost our connection to books and the wonder of imagination evoked through great storytelling.

If you are a musician, pull out the guitar, drums, violin, flute, or other instrument and have a sing-along. One of life's great joys is gathering everyone together in the living room and singing songs. Pick up some songbooks that everyone would enjoy. Who said disasters were all work and no fun? Actually, Y2K could truly bring us closer than we've ever been.

F. Moving

As you prepare for the Y2K crisis I'm sure you've recognized the fact that nobody knows exactly where and how it will affect us. That's why one of the toughest questions of Y2K preparedness is whether it's safe to stay where you are, or should you move?

After reading this book, you should recognize that living in a tiny apartment without any outdoor space gives you the most limited preparedness options. Storing large amounts of food and water will be a problem, and installing a woodstove is not an option. Without being able to store a propane gas tank outside, a propane gas heater or stove is useless. A few apartment owners, however, are taking the Y2K crisis seriously enough to install propane heating systems for their buildings. Find out how your apartment managers plan to provide heat in a power outage. Talk to friends to see if you can work together to get a country house outfitted for Y2K emergencies, and arrange to go there to ride out the Y2K crisis. There's no need to panic. By reaching out, you may find you have many more options. Working together you can save your money by sharing resources, supplies, and equipment.

G. Working Through the Kinks

Once you get Y2K preparations in place, conduct practices with the family. Shut off the electricity to see how everything works and where there are holes in your plan. Try not to cheat, but if you do, its probably because some areas need additional attention. For example, you may find that you need more lights because people wanted to go to bed at different times, and it caused friction over who got to use the lighting.

H. Talking to Kids About Y2K

Our children are smarter than we think. It's important to include them in your Y2K preparedness plans and efforts. Some parents are even finding out about Y2K from their kids, not the other way around. And hey, maybe it will shake off some of your kids' bad habits like watching too much TV or staying up late playing video games.

Computers are as much a part of kids' lives as bicycles and TV, so they may feel more comfortable with technology than grown-ups. For us, learning about computers has been a little like trying to learn Spanish in college, whereas kids have learned the "language" of computers at a fresh impressionable age when everything is just soaked up. Children today have nò experience in a world without computers, so it's easier for them to truly understand how dependent society is on technology. The fact that kids are so familiar with computers helps when explaining Y2K and the problems that will result. Don't underestimate your child's ability to understand Y2K and its consequences as you share and involve them in your preparedness plans.

The most important message you can convey to your children is that Y2K is not going to bring the end of the world and that they are going to be okay. Assure them that even though some weird things may happen for a while, like the power going out or having to be careful only to drink stored water, they'll be safe. Certainly, there's no reason to raise concerns where there are none, but the older the child, the more aware and sensitive he or she may be to your fears. Explain to them that by preparing for any emergency, whether it's Y2K or a hurricane, the whole family will be safer and more comfortable.

Get the kids involved in helping you prepare. Kids can be awfully good sports if they want to be, and besides, you can make it fun. After all, emergency preparedness has a lot in common with camping, and most kids love that! Have them help you fill and store water jugs. If you have a home dehydrator, get them to slice fruits and/or place them on the tray for dehydrating. Older kids can stack some firewood and learn how to build a fire and split logs for kindling.

Some teenagers and young adults may be more cynical than younger kids and find the prospects of Y2K breakdowns an overall intrusion into their busy lives. Nonetheless, try to involve them in the preparedness process, too. One mother wrote us recently about her daughter's attitude adjustment after learning how to prepare for Y2K: "My daughter, who has bounced between acceptance and anger about how Y2K may disrupt her life plans, said, 'Hmmm, somehow [after learning how to prepare for Y2K], I don't feel so scared anymore... it helps me to see that this is doable.' "

Without alarming them, go through the various aspects of emergency preparedness with your children. The best thing to do is to actually test your preparedness by scheduling a family emergency drill night. On the designated night, turn off all the power in the house (except maybe the refrigerator, so you don't ruin food), and see what happens. You all may get a better understanding of what's to come when suddenly, there's no TV, no heat, no lights, and the stove or microwave don't work. You'll find out very quickly how conditioned you are to having electricity. By doing an emergency drill, you'll see the holes in your plan, and the kids will experience firsthand what a Y2K emergency could mean.

Regardless of how involved your kids get, stress the importance of safety. Let's highlight some key points to make with kids about things to do or look out for in a Y2K emergency:

- ▸ **Water** Explain that because of the Y2K bug, water out of the kitchen or bathroom faucet may not be safe to drink on New Year's Day and for awhile afterward. Let them know that they should only drink the water that you have stored or treated. That includes brushing their teeth, too. Show them what the water containers look like and where they are stored.

- ▸ **Food** Teach your kids good food storage habits. Obviously, you want your food to last as long as possible, so explain how important it is that foods are resealed well. This means to do things like putting lids back on jars and containers securely to keep air and moisture out, carefully folding the inside liner bag of cereal boxes, etc. Basically, the rule is, "If you opened it, seal it back up, too." Also, emphasize not wasting food. Only pour, serve, or dig into what they're going to eat. Let them know food supplies are limited. Discuss alternate cooking plans. If the power goes out, and you have to use a camp stove, explain the dangers of open flame burners.

- ▸ **Emergency Services** Review emergency procedures you

probably have already taught your kids: how to call the police, the fire department and the doctor—with a couple of minor differences. For one thing, since Y2K problems will occur on a *set date*, January 1, make sure phone numbers are posted by the phone in plain sight for kids to see, The list should include numbers for the police department, fire department, doctor's office, hospital, water department, and power company. The phones may not work and emergency services could be very limited, but it's better to have the numbers there just in case. Remember, a child could save your life.

▸ **Heat** Alternate sources of heat and light often mean added danger of fire, especially with kids around. A woodstove can look very inviting but poses potential for serious burns. Candles, of course, are a handy alternate light source but are a huge fire danger and for that reason are not a good emergency solution. However, inevitably, people will use them, so children have to be very careful not to ever knock a candle over.

In addition, emergency heating and lighting sources often use gas fuels, which can be dangerous. Teach children what fuel or gasoline smells like so that they know never to light a match or lighter when such odors are present.

While Y2K may bring serious disruptions to the daily routines of work, school, and shopping, it may bring out the kindness and generosity of neighbors and strangers. Hopefully there won't be major disruptions, but if there are, it might be a blessing to miss work for a few days and stay home with the kids to play games and cook big stews. Kids suffer the most from frenetic work lives of their parents. The possible disruption of our daily lives may be the best thing that happens to your family.

CHECKLISTS

To-Do List for the first week of December 1999

_____ Collect all final financial and personal records (i.e., bank statements, credit card statements, etc.) *See Financial/ Personal Checklist.*

_____ Review all checklists to make sure you haven't forgotten any essential items.

_____ Conduct a preparedness practice with the family.

_____ Test your battery-powered carbon monoxide and smoke detectors. Replace batteries immediately, if necessary.

To-Do List for the last week of December 1999

_____ Stock up on fresh foods and produce to get as far into the new year as possible.

_____ Check stored water inventory (1 gallon per person per day, at least).

_____ Get last-minute prescriptions filled.

_____ Check fuel supplies for camp stoves, grills, kerosene or propane heaters, generators, and lanterns.

_____ Charge all rechargeable batteries.

_____ Wash dirty clothes.

To-Do List for December 30 and 31, 1999:

_____ Fill bathtubs and available storage bottles with water.

_____ Fill the car(s) with gas.

_____ Take out the trash.

_____ Buy or make as much ice as you can store in refrigerator and coolers.

Food Storage Checklist

Grocery Shopping List to guide you as to what foods to store from the supermarket and food reserve companies.

CANNED GOODS

Meats
_____ Fish (tuna, mackerel, oysters, sardines, salmon)
_____ Poultry (chicken, turkey)
_____ Red meat (ham, Spam, sausages)
_____ Soups

Vegetables and Fruits
_____ Tomatoes
_____ Tomato sauce and paste
_____ Peas, green beans
_____ Spinach
_____ Potatoes
_____ Squash
_____ Asparagus
_____ Peaches, fruit cocktail, and pears. (Acidic fruits don't last as long so purchase these items last and use first.)
_____ Applesauce
_____ Bottled fruit juices
_____ Prunes, raisins, and other dried fruits
_____ Corn
_____ Mushrooms
_____ Beets
_____ Lemon juice
_____ Dried bananas

Dry Goods

(Remember, boxed goods store about six to twelve months only)

_____ Grains and beans (wheat, lentils, millet, couscous, kidney beans, etc.)

_____ Sprouting seeds (lentils, alfalfa, radish, mung beans, etc.)

_____ Rice (instant and brown)

_____ Powdered milk

_____ Evaporated milk

_____ Powdered eggs

_____ Cheese powder

_____ Nonhybrid seeds for sprouting (mung, lentils, alfalfa, clover, sunflower, etc.)

_____ Macaroni and cheese

_____ Bouillon cubes

_____ Nondairy creamer

_____ Pastas

_____ Breakfast cereals

_____ Crackers

_____ Peanut Butter

_____ Pudding/Jell-O

_____ Pancake mix

_____ Snack food—chips, cookies

_____ Candy (hard candy stores indefinitely)

_____ Soy nuts

_____ Nuts

_____ Coffee and tea

_____ Sodas

_____ Dried onions

_____ Bay leaves (these will also help keep bugs out of flour and grains)

_____ Ketchup and mustard

_____ Salt and pepper

_____ Herbs and spices

_____ Sugar

_____ Baking powder

_____ Baking soda
_____ Olive oil and other oils
_____ Yeast
_____ Wine
_____ Cocoa
_____ Vinegar

Food From Food Reserve Companies

These supplies should be ordered immediately as demand is high and food reserve companies often need two to four months lead time for delivery.

_____ Freeze-dried foods
_____ Dehydrated foods
_____ MREs (Typically sold in cases of twelve meals)

Special Diets

Consider special needs such as food for infants or the elderly. Nursing mothers may need liquid formula in case they are unable to nurse. Canned dietetic foods, juices, and soups may be helpful for the ill and elderly.

Pets

_____ Two to three months of pet food
_____ Kitty litter
_____ Flea collars
_____ Animal tags with address and phone number
_____ Bird seed or other animal food
_____ Miscellaneous pet supplies (i.e., leash, chew toys, etc.)

Items to Purchase in the Last Couple of Weeks

Fresh Foods
_____ Potatoes
_____ Onions and garlic
_____ Squash
_____ Fresh fruits and vegetables
_____ Yogurt for base culture

Storage Supplies
_____ Oxygen absorbers
_____ Large plastic buckets (with screw top lids)
_____ Plastic containers (with lids, various sizes)
_____ Impulse sealer (with foil pouches to extend shelf life of food)
_____ Glass jars and canning lids

Kitchen Equipment and Supplies Checklist

Many of these things you probably already have or would never use, emergency or not, but just to make sure you've thought everything through, you can use this as a handy guide.

_____ Paper plates and plastic utensils/cups (to reduce the need for washing dishes)
_____ Paper towels and napkins
_____ Cookbooks
_____ Nonelectric can opener
_____ Disposable utensils
_____ Pots and pans—variety of sizes
_____ Coffee filters
_____ Aluminum foil (better than dirtying pans)
_____ Scouring pads
_____ Heavy-duty Zip-lock bags of all sizes
_____ Thermoses
_____ Measuring cups/spoons
_____ Dehydrator

_____ Flour sifter
_____ Cooler
_____ Funnel
_____ Rubber gloves
_____ Sharp knives
_____ Grater
_____ Tea kettle
_____ Hand slicer
_____ Cheesecloth (for sprouting)
_____ Potato masher
_____ Spatulas and ladle
_____ Hand juicer
_____ Baby bottles and disposable baby bottle liners
_____ Trash bags
_____ Timer
_____ Wisk
_____ Egg beater
_____ Strainer
_____ Sprouting kit
_____ Safety matches

Water Preparation Checklist

_____ Water storage containers (enough for one gallon per person per day for fourteen days)
_____ Water filter or purifier
_____ Extra filters for water filter
_____ Bleach and eye-dropper
_____ Iodine tablets
_____ Water hose and siphon tube

Heating, Cooking, and Lighting Checklists

Heating

_____ Wood for fireplace or woodstove, kindling for one month
_____ Fuels for heaters, stoves, and lanterns

_____ Stove "generator" device ($15—$20)
_____ Extra wicks for kerosene stoves
_____ Battery-operated carbon monoxide and smoke detectors (for any flame-burning device)
_____ Fireplace tools

Cooking
_____ Dual-fuel camp stove
_____ Kerosene gas stove
_____ Propane fuel for outdoor gas grill
_____ Alco-brite canisters
_____ Battery-operated carbon monoxide and smoke detectors (For any flame-burning device)

Lighting

GAS LANTERNS
_____ Battery-operated carbon monoxide and smoke detectors (for any flame-burning device)
_____ Lanterns—(two or three minimum)
_____ Coleman fuel
_____ Lots of extra mantels
_____ Spare fuel caps and a lantern generator
_____ An extra glass globe per lamp
_____ A sparker (comes separately as an attachment)

PROPANE LANTERNS
_____ Several Propane Disposable bottles
_____ Lots of extra mantels

KEROSENE LANTERNS
_____ Kerosene fuel
_____ Glass chimney
_____ Lots of mantels
_____ Wall brackets (optional)

BATTERY LANTERNS
_____ Extra alkaline batteries
_____ Rechargeable nicad batteries and charger

OTHER LIGHTS
_____ Fluorescent light bulbs
_____ Maglight flashlight
_____ Rechargeable batteries for flashlights
_____ Light sticks
_____ Long-burning candles (as back-up only)

BATTERY AND BATTERY INVERTER SYSTEM
_____ Deep cycle battery or Boost-It Power Pak unit
_____ Battery inverter with enough wattage rating to handle your needs
_____ Solar panel or generator to recharge battery

GENERATORS
_____ Gas and gas containers for gas generator
_____ Fill propane tank for propane generator
_____ Oil and air filters
_____ Extension power cords

Health

Medical and Dental To-do Lists
_____ Have all medical and dental work done well before January 1, 2000
_____ Extra prescription glasses
_____ Copies of prescription records
_____ Extra medications (at least two to three months supply)
_____ Proof of payment for health insurance
_____ Immunization records
_____ First-aid kit

Personal and Family Hygiene Checklist

_____ Toothpaste and toothbrushes

_____ Soap and detergent

_____ Towels and washcloths

_____ Nail clippers

_____ Mirrors, combs, and brushes

_____ Mouthwash

_____ Toilet paper and tissues

_____ Shampoo

_____ Prescription medications, aspirin, etc.

_____ Vaseline

_____ Chapstick

_____ Lotions

_____ Feminine supplies

_____ Contraceptives

_____ Deodorant

_____ Room deodorizer

_____ Disinfectants for cleaning/sanitation

_____ Eye dropper

_____ Diapers and other baby needs

_____ Denture needs (cream, adhesive, and cleaning solution)

_____ Razor blades and shaving cream

_____ Hair clippers

_____ Ear plugs

_____ Q-tips

_____ Toilet plunger

_____ Solar shower

_____ Chlorine bleach (5.25% sodium hypochlorite as only active ingredient, with no soap or other additives)

Nonprescriptive Supplies Checklist

_____ Kleenex

_____ Face masks

_____ Hot water bottle

_____ Vitamin and mineral supplements

_____ Lozenges

_____ Aspirin, Tylenol, and Advil
_____ Sunscreen
_____ Anti-diarrhea medications
_____ Anti-fungal cream
_____ Allergy and asthma medications
_____ Safety pins
_____ Antacid
_____ Laxative
_____ Cold and flu medication
_____ Insect repellent

First-Aid Kit Checklist
_____ First-aid manual
_____ Hydrogen peroxide
_____ Ace bandages
_____ Dermaplast (topical anesthetic)
_____ Triple antibiotic ointment
_____ Cleansing agent and sterile soap
_____ Eye dropper
_____ Cottonballs
_____ Epsom salts
_____ Enema equipment
_____ Ice pack
_____ First-aid cream or Silvadene
_____ Disposable gloves
_____ Cortisporin ophthalmic solution
_____ Syrup of Ipecac
_____ Iodine
_____ Bed pan
_____ Rubbing alcohol
_____ Q-tips
_____ Sterile adhesive strips
_____ Band-Aids
_____ Sterile gauze pads (various sizes)
_____ Activated charcoal
_____ Antiseptic spray

_____ Eye wash
_____ Hypoallergenic adhesive tape
_____ Latex gloves
_____ Moistened towelettes
_____ Needles
_____ Razor blades
_____ Vaseline
_____ Safety pins
_____ Scissors
_____ Thermometer
_____ Tongue depressors
_____ Triangular bandages
_____ Tube petroleum jelly
_____ Tweezers
_____ Tourniquet

Sanitation and Refuse Checklist

_____ Extra garbage cans with tight-fitting lids
_____ Ammonia
_____ Lots of large trash bags
_____ Detergent
_____ Disinfectant spray
_____ Washboard
_____ Composter (optional)
_____ Insect traps and bug spray
_____ Sponges and mop
_____ Brillo pads
_____ Broom and dustpan
_____ Buckets
_____ Bleach
_____ Ajax

Baby Supplies Checklist

_____ Baby foods
_____ Bottles and nipples

_____ Diapers
_____ Formula, powdered milk, and juices
_____ Prescription medications (if any)

Clothing and Bedding Checklist

_____ Blankets and sleeping bag
_____ Poncho
_____ Raincoat and umbrella
_____ Sturdy shoes and/or work boots
_____ Sturdy work clothes and/or overalls
_____ Hat, gloves, ear muffs, and scarf
_____ Thermal underwear
_____ Warm socks
_____ Clothesline

Tools Checklist

_____ Tool boxes or bags
_____ Tape measure
_____ Hammer
_____ Oil can
_____ Nails (wide variety)
_____ Rope
_____ Screws (wide variety)
_____ Hooks (wide variety)
_____ Utility knife
_____ Shovel
_____ Complete set of screwdrivers
_____ Complete set of chisels
_____ Pipe wrenches (various sizes)
_____ Ladder
_____ Crescent wrenches (various sizes)
_____ Square
_____ Duct tape
_____ Glue
_____ WD-40

_____ Caulk gun and silicone caulk
_____ Hand saws
_____ Needlenose pliers
_____ Gloves
_____ Wood-cutting Ax
_____ Hand mower
_____ Staple gun and staples
_____ Rope, cord, and twine
_____ Water hoses
_____ Roll of plastic
_____ Extension cords
_____ Jumper cables
_____ Car oil and air filters
_____ Fishing gear
_____ Compass
_____ Garden tools (clippers, hoe, trowel, etc.)

Miscellaneous Home Supplies and Entertainment

_____ Board games, cards, puzzles
_____ Camera with lots of film
_____ Typewriter
_____ Laptop computer with solar panel power unit
_____ Pencils, pens
_____ Glue and scissors
_____ Pads of writing paper, rubber bands, calculator, and tape measure
_____ Needles, thread, and other sewing supplies
_____ Fabric to make and repair clothes
_____ Yarn and knitting needles
_____ Books (novels, preparedness manuals, health and medical texts, cookbooks, etc.)
_____ Home schooling materials
_____ Skis, sleds, snowshoes, and toboggans
_____ Baseball and bat, basketball, and tennis racket and balls

_____ Art supplies (easel, paints, crayons, clay, color pencils, pastels, etc.)
_____ Musical instruments and supplies
_____ Songbooks

Financial and Personal Documents
_____ Bank statements and recent deposit slips, canceled checks that show proof of payment, mortgage payment statements
_____ Credit card statements and account numbers
_____ Insurance policies
_____ Wills
_____ Deeds and contracts
_____ Stocks and bonds
_____ Passports
_____ Social Security cards
_____ Family records (birth, marriage, and death certificates)
_____ Inventory of valuable household goods and important telephone numbers

Communications and Security
_____ Wind-up or solar radio
_____ Walkie-talkies
_____ Small TV
_____ Solar outdoor lights

PREPAREDNESS SUPPLIERS

Food

Essentials 2000   (800) 775-1991
PO Box 158   www.essentials2000.com
Nevada City, CA 95959   sales@essentials2000.com

They carry top-of-the-line freeze-dried and dehydrated food including
Alpine Aire and Mountain House. They have a wonderful variety of
ready-made entrées, individual items (corn, beans, fruits, milk, etc.), and
complete one-year kits. There is a quick turnaround on complete food
packages or à la carte. This company is owned and operated by Denis
Korn, a highly respected expert on preparedness food and a twenty-five-
year veteran in the industry. They also carry emergency supplies like
water purifiers, oxygen absorbers (for food preservation), and radios.
(GET SPECIAL 5% DISCOUNT IF YOU MENTION "NIMOY" BOOK)

Millennium III Foods   (888) 883-1603
PO Box 10010   www.m3mfoods.com
Bozeman, MT 59719

They get their food directly from growers so shortages are rare. They
have restaurant quality dehydrated food that is packed in #10 cans for
long-term storage. These foods contain no MSG, few preservatives, and
no fillers. They offer great prices, and can deliver in roughly two weeks.
As CEO Carole Munson says, "There is never a need to eat survival food.
Eat the way you always do."
(GET SPECIAL 5% DISCOUNT IF YOU MENTION "NIMOY" BOOK)

The Ark Institute
PO Box 142
Oxford, OH 45056

(800) 255-1912
www.arkinstitute.com

They carry a comprehensive Y2K preparedness package of nonhybrid seeds. They also have a wonderful collection of gardening and preparedness books.
(GET SPECIAL 5% DISCOUNT IF YOU MENTION "NIMOY" BOOK)

Health

Hospital-in-a-Box
Family Physicians Home
   Emergency Company
PO Box 211205
Bedford, TX 76095

(877) 326-7497

Hospital-in-a-Box comes with 1,200 medical supplies, a video, and a manual that guides you through a wide variety of medical problems. It's expensive at $795, but it is worth it. Family Physicians Home Emergency Company also carries some good books: *First Aid and Emergency Procedures* ($29.95) and *Your Personal Y2K Medical Preparation Plan* ($21.95).

Water Purification

General Ecology
151 Sheree Blvd.
Exton, PA 19341

(800) 441-8166 (U.S. only)
(for local dealers) (610) 363-7900
www.general-ecology.com

General

Jade Mountain   (800) 442-1972
PO Box 4616
Boulder, CO 80306-4616

They carry a complete line of preparedness equipment: water purifiers, gas heaters, solar gear, lanterns, and much more. They hold a self-sustainable living philosophy. Their store is located in Boulder, Colorado. You can order a catalog or equipment by calling the toll-free number. (WHEN ORDERING PRODUCTS, MENTION #SA300)

Real Goods Trading Company   (800) 762-7325
555 Leslie St.   FAX (800) 508-2342
Ukiah, CA 95482-5576

They stock a complete line of preparedness equipment: water purifiers, gas heaters, solar gear, lanterns and much more. They hold a self-sustainable living philosophy. They have stores in Berkeley and Hopland, California, and Eugene, Oregon.

Major Surplus And Supply   (800) 441-8855
435 W. Alondra Blvd.
Gardena, CA 90248

They have a very knowledgeable staff and a complete line of camping and preparedness equipment and supplies.

Multisorb Industries   888-SORBENT

PORTA-POWER BOOST IT PACK BATTERY AND INVERTER

Sun Solar Systems

www.webaccess.net/~sunsolar
systems
SunSolarSystems@webaccess
.net

FINANCIAL RESOURCES

William T. Hepburn, CFP,
  President
Hepburn & Associates
805 Whipple St.
Suite C
Prescott, AZ 86301

(520) 778-4000
whepburn@primenet.com

Books to Add to Your Preparedness Library

Alternative Energy
The Independent Home—Living Well with Power from the Sun, Wind and Water
By Michael Potts
Order from Real Goods—(800) 919-2400
($19.95)

Real Goods' *Solar Living Sourcebook*
By John Schaeffer and Real Goods Staff
Order from Real Goods—(800) 919-2400
($24.95)

Y2K Financial Books/Newsletters
How to Profit From the Y2K Recession
By John Mauldin

Learn how to *make* money with Y2K as you protect your assets. This is a serious book on wise investing by well-respected financial investment analyst John Mauldin.
Available in bookstores and at Amazon.com.
($24.95)

Year 2000 Alert
by Weiss Research
Stay up to date on Y2K investment strategies with this monthly newsletter.
Order direct—(800) 317-6278
($98 for 12 issues)

Cookbooks for Stored Foods

Cooking with Home Storage
by Peggy Layton and Vicki Tate
Order from Major Surplus and Supply—(800) 441-8855
($15.95)

Just Add Water
by Barbara Salsbury
Order from Major Surplus and Supply—(800) 441-8855
($15.95)

Both of these easy to read books are just what you need for dehydrated foods. They have lots of recipes and advice on putting together a food storage plan with dehydrated foods out of the Mormon tradition. Take your pick or get both.

Gardening Books

How to Grow More Vegetables, Fruits, Nuts, Berries, Grains and Other Crops (On Less Land Than You Ever Thought Possible)
by John Jeavons

This book is a classic in home gardening and a must for anyone wanting to make the most of their edible gardens. It shows how to raise fresh healthy vegetables for a family of four on any tiny patch of land whether on a flat rooftop or a small section of ground by your house.
Available in bookstores and at Amazon.com
($13.55)

Burpee: The Complete Vegetable & Herb Gardener: A Guide to Growing Your Garden Organically
by Karan Davis Cutler
This book focuses on all aspects of growing organic vegetables and edible herbs in the home garden. It includes planting techniques, tools, garden design, and more than 90 individual plant portraits, as well as 300 full-color photos.
Available in bookstores and at Amazon.com.
($19.95)

Rodale's All-New Encyclopedia of Organic Gardening: The Indispensable Resource for Every Gardener
by Marshall Bradley

This all-new, authoritative edition of the 1978 classic, which sold more than 625,000 copies, provides practical, up-to-date information for every gardener, beginner and veteran alike.
Available in bookstores and at Amazon.com.
($19.95)

Y2K Information Prepardness

Web site Resources

Use the Internet! Driven by concerns of public panic, the mainstream media has largely soft-pedaled the seriousness of Y2K. With a few exceptions, many government and business leaders have chosen to ignore Y2K for fear that they could in some way be held accountable for it. For these reasons and more, the Internet has become an invaluable resource for the latest news, reports, and information about Y2K.

The following list provides Web sites covering a broad spectrum of issues about Y2K. Most of these Web sites also provide additional links to many other useful Y2K sites.

Y2K News and Information Resources:

www.nimoy2k.com
This is the author's Web site that lists updates of the latest information from Y2K experts and tips on Y2K preparedness.

www.y2kwatch.com
This Web site offers free e-mail with updates, editorial commentary, and general information.

www.y2ktoday.com
An excellent source of Y2K information, this is a clearinghouse of Y2K articles from major media outlets covering all aspects of the problem.

www.year2000.com
Peter deJager's site is called the Paul Revere of Y2K. It also has informative e-mail lists you can join.

www.worldnetdaily.com
It's an excellent source of Y2K news.

www.y2ktimebomb.com
It contains many Y2K media articles.

www.yourdon.com
This is Ed Yourdon's site. He wrote the *New York Times* best-seller, *Timebomb 2000*. One of the world's leading experts in computer software, he has written twenty-five books about computers and is very knowledgeable about the possible millennium bug impact.

www.euy2k.com
This is the best source for information on the electric utility companies. It is the site of Rick Cowles, author of *Electric Utilities and Y2K*.

www.rx2000.org
This site is the best source for information regarding health care and Y2K.

Community Y2K Organizing & Preparedness

www.cassandraproject.org
The Cassandra Project, the most well-known personal preparedness site. Offers preparedness information and community Y2K group contact information.

www.redcross.org/disaster/safety/y2k.html
This is the Red Cross' Web site on Y2K preparedness.

www.y2kwomen.com
This is an excellent site for Y2K information targeted to women. It covers psychological and emotional issues, as well as preparedness. It is run by Y2K speaker Karen Anderson.

Financial and Economic Issues

www.yardeni.com
Ed Yardeni is the Chief Economist of Deutsche Bank Securities and international economic adviser on Y2K. Read his "Y2K Notebook" and other economic information and updates.

www.fdic.gov/about/y2k
This site contains updates and information on the banking industry and Y2K.

www.2000wave.com
John Mauldin is author of *How to Profit from the Y2K Recession* and editor of the "Year 2000 Alert" newsletter. This site offers tips and latest Y2K information.

Government Y2K info

www.house.gov/reform/gmit/y2k/
Representative Steve Horn, Chairman of the House Subcommittee on Management and Technology, reports on Y2K progress.

www.senate.gov/~bennett
Senator Robert Bennett, (R-Utah) is the Year 2000 Committee Chairman.

APPENDIX 1
Y2K CALENDAR OF KEY SPIKE DATES

We all know about the problems computers will have when reading the Year 2000. There are, however, several other date-sensitive days that can and will cause some degree of problems leading up to and following January 1, 2000. For example, dates that have the numbers "99" might be problematic due to the fact that sometimes programmers use the numbers "99" to indicate the end of a file or to quit a program. Other particularly sensitive dates are those that fall on days when city, state, or local governments begin their fiscal year and in effect, are projecting into the Year 2000.

The following are Y2K "spike" dates to track in the future:

- June 30, 1999—Securities and Exchange Commission requires that publicly traded companies report on their current "state of (Y2K) readiness" including the costs of making any corrections. They also need to include the "worst-case" scenarios and how they would handle them.
- July 1, 1999—Fiscal year begins for forty-six states. Also, this is the Nuclear Regulatory Commission deadline for nuclear power plants to prove Y2K compliance.
- September 9, 1999—9/9/99 is used as a stop date on some programs. Some computers could read this number as a halt command.

- September 30, 1999—SEC requires that publicly traded companies report on their current "state of (Y2K) readiness" including the costs of making any corrections. They also need to include the "worst-case" scenarios and how they would handle them.
- October 1, 1999—Fiscal Year 2000 begins for the federal government, Alabama, and Michigan.
- January 1, 2000—Y2K's D-Day, the granddaddy of all Y2K "spike" dates. Also, if embedded chips fail, they will fail on this day. It falls on a Saturday, which is widely seen as a good thing.
- January 3, 2000—First day back at work in the New Year. Many computers will experience their first problems as they encounter their first "00" when they are booted up.
- February 29, 2000—Years that end in "00" usually aren't leap years unless they are a multiple of four, like 2000. This has been overlooked by many computer programmers and is likely to cause many program errors.

APPENDIX 2
Ed Yardeni Speaks Out

From a knowledgeable and respected insider's position, Ed Yardeni, Chief Economist of Deutsche Bank Securities and international economic adviser on Y2K, spells out why Y2K remediation will fail in so many sectors of government and business. Read Yardeni's complete Y2K Netbook on the Internet at www.yardeni.com.

Mission Critical Approach Guarantees Failure

The U.S. government's approach to fixing Y2K seems to be the way everyone else is approaching this problem. This approach is bound to fail. The current Y2K global battle plan has at least seven major flaws:

1) **Unorganized**—For starters, there is no plan. If there is one, it certainly isn't global at all, or even national. It is highly decentralized. Each company and government agency is responsible for fixing Y2K on its own. There are few industry alliances working to solve the problem collectively. Fixing and responding to the Y2K problem requires a cooperative approach.

2) **Unaware**—There is no global campaign to maximize awareness of Y2K, and very few national efforts to alert the public.

3) **Uncontrolled**—Each Y2K-fixing entity independently establishes a triage process to identify mission-critical versus noncritical systems. No authority, regulator, or industry association has defined the meaning of—or established standards for—the widely misused term "mission critical."

4) **Unverified**—Available resources are focused on fixing mission-critical systems, however defined. Y2K managers are free to reclassify mission-critical systems as noncritical. They might do this under the increasing pressure of the looming deadline to show more progress than is in fact possible to achieve. There is simply too little independent verification of progress. [The total number of federal government mission-critical systems dropped from 8,589 to 7,850 over the three-month reporting period in 1998 because of reclassification. The Department of Defense reduced its mission-critical systems count from 3,143 to 2,915.]

5) **Unprotected**—Computer systems exchange data all the time. Information systems and databases may easily be contaminated by data received from noncompliant Y2K systems.

6) **Untested**—Even fixed systems could fail once they are tested in "real time." Most embedded chip systems probably won't be tested, let alone be fixed, in time for the century date change.

7) **Unaccountable**—It is up to managers to decide whether to fix noncritical systems or to let them fail in 2000. Without a cooperative or collective approach, it is likely that some managers won't fix some noncritical systems that are actually mission critical. There is no standard for these managers to measure up to.

This last point is crucially important. It is the ground zero of the potential Y2K explosion. We all need to know if the products, services, information, orders, jobs, incomes, and payments that we depend on have been doomed by the triage decisions of those who provide them. If so, we might already be toast in 2000 and not know it.

Next time someone tells you that they've 1) identified their mission-critical systems 2) are fixing the ones that are noncompliant, and 3) expect to finish testing in time to implement them before January 1, 2000, ask them to tell you about their noncompliant noncritical systems that won't be fixed and are expected to blow up starting on that fateful date.

INDEX

AC power/inverters, 72, 77, 84, 159
Airline travel, 157–158
Apartments, 164
Appliances, 36, 73
ATMs, 153
Atrazine, 49

Baby, *see infant*
Baby supplies checklist, 178–179
Banking industry, 65, 146
Banks
   lack of resources, 140, 146, 155
   run on, 146
   safety deposit boxes, 143–144
   safety ratings, obtaining, 141
   statements/deposit slips, 142, 143
   vaults, 161
Batteries, 73, 78–84, 112–116, 159, 162
   car, 80
   deep cycle, 80–81, 85
   Porta-Power Boost It Pack, 82–84
Battery charger, 114
Battery inverter, 71, 81–82, 162
Battery lantern, 112, 115
Beans, 12, 29, 36
Bennett, Senator Robert, iii, xvii, 192
Blackouts, 66, 67, 68
Bonds, 146, 150, 151
Books, 187–189
Brownouts, 66, 67
   tips about, 68

Bulk foods, 8, 16–17
   storage of, 32–33, 34
Burns, Sherry, 120

Camping stoves, *see gas stoves*
Candles, 117–118, 167
Canned goods, 11, 18, 28, 34, 35
Carbon monoxide detectors, 91, 92, 108
Cars, 157
Cassandra Project Web site, 93, 189
Checklists
   baby supplies, 178–179
   clothing and bedding, 179
   communications and security, 181
   financial and personal documents,
     181
   first-aid kit, 177–178
   food storage, 169–171
   heating, cooking, and lighting,
     173–175
   kitchen sundries, 172–173
   medical and dental to-do, 175
   miscellaneous home supplies and
     entertainment, 180–181
   nonprescriptive (medical) supplies,
     176–177
   personal and family hygiene, 176
   sanitation and refuse, 178
   to-do, 168
   tools, 179–180
   water preparation, 173

Chemical light sticks, 118
Children, and special needs of, 42, 129, 164–167
Chlorine, 49, 57–58, 60
CIA, Year 2000 Office, 120
Civil unrest & rioting, 160
Clothing and bedding checklist, 179
Coal, 64
Coins, 154–155
Coleman
  coolers, 105
  lanterns, 107–108, 112, 115
  stoves and fuel, 95–97
Community, 93
Communications, 159
Communications and security
  checklist, 181
Computers, failing of and effects on
  billing systems, 41
  electrical power shortage/outage, 39, 40, 46, 51, 59 , 63–65, 67–69, 146, 153, 157, 160
  entitlement checks, 160
  financial records, 142
  food inventory & distribution, 2–3, 63
  water treatment plants, 39, 46, 60
Computer contamination, 194
Cooking, 68, 72, 94
  cookbooks, 186
  essentials & condiments, 15
  heating, cooking, and lighting
    checklist, 173–175
  *also see kitchen supplies &
    equipment*
Cookstoves, 90, 91
Coolers, 105
CPR, 123–124
Credit cards, 142–143, 154
Credit unions, 140
Cryptosporidium, 48, 51, 57, 58
Curtiss, Michael, 141

Dairy, 27, 28
DC power, 81
Debt, 154
Dehydrated foods, 6–7, 9, 18–19, 21–22, 28, 29, 36
  advantages/disadvantages of, 22
  compared to freeze-dried, 20
  storage of, 33, 34, 35
Deflation, 147, 155
Deutsche Bank Securities, 146
Dirty power, *see brownouts*
Documents/records, 142–144, 155, 161
Dodd, Senator Christopher, xix, 62
Dow Jones Industrial Average, 147, 149
Duel-fuel stoves, 95–97
Dry foods, 11–12

Elderly, special needs of, 16, 93, 130
Electricity, lack of, *see computers*
Embedded microchips, 3, 40, 64, 157, 194
Emergency drill, 166
Entertainment, 162–163
Entertainment checklist, 180
Energy conservation, 69–72
EPA, 52
Extension cords, 76

FDA, 130–131
FDIC, 145, 146, 148
Federal Aviation Administration
  (FAA), 157
Federal Reserve, 141, 144, 145, 146
Financial and personal documents
  checklist, 183
Financial preparedness, 153–155
Financial records, 142–144, 155
Fireplaces, 87, 138
First-aid, 124, 125–128
  abrasions, 125

First-aid (*continued*)
  blisters, 126
  bleeding, 126
  swelling, 126
  compression dressing, 127
  eye injuries, 127
  poisoning, 128
First-aid kits, 124, 125
First-aid kit checklist, 177–178
Flashlights, 115–117, 159
Fluorescent lightbulbs, 71–72, 112
Foil, 33, 36
Fondue pots, 102
Food inventory & distribution, 2–4, 146
Food storage
  cookbooks, 186
  food reserves, 18–24
  food storage checklist, 169–172
  food storage kit, 18
  foods to store, 6–31
  mistakes with, 35
  planning, 4–6, 27–31
  preparedness foods comparison
    chart, 8–9
  preparedness examples &
    suggestions chart, 25–26
  proper storage, 31–35
  tips, 35, 166
Freeze-dried foods, 6–7, 8, 18, 19, 28,
  29
  advantages/disadvantages of, 21
  sample costs chart, 20
  storage of, 33, 34–35
Fuel, solid, 101–102
Fuel, storage of, 74, 91–92
Fuels, comparing, 99–101

Garbage, 138–139
Gardening, 30–31, 186–187
Gas
  gasoline, 74, 78, 91, 95, 96, 157, 160,
    168
  compared to kerosene, 100–101
  natural gas, 64, 162

Gas heaters/stoves, 89, 94
  camping, 95–99
  comparing fuels for stoves chart,
    100–101
Gas lanterns, 106–111
General Ecology Company, 51, 53–54
Generator, 68, 71, 72, 73–74, 75
  cost of, 76
  generator wattage chart, 77–78
  recharging batteries, 79
Giardia, 48, 51
Grains, 12–13, 29, 33, 36
Grain mills, 37
Greenspan, Alan, 146
Grills, 101
Grocery stores, 1
Gun, 160

Health care & emergency services
  limited access to, 120–121
  medical planning, 122–125
  medical records, 123
  nonprescriptive supplies checklist,
    176–177
  pharmaceutical drugs &
    prescriptions, 123
  self-reliance, 121–122, 166–168
Heating, 68, 69, 72, 85, 86, 87–94, 167
Heating, cooking, and lighting
  checklist, 173–175
Herbs, 130–131, 133–136
  herbal health kit chart, 134–136
Home supplies checklist, 180, 181
Hospitals, 67
Hot water system, 85
Hygiene, personal & family, 136–137

Illness, and special needs of, 42, 93
The Independent Home, by Michael
  Potts, 86
Infants, special needs of, 16, 42
  (colic), 129
Inflation, 152

Insulation, 70, 90
Insurance companies, 140, 154
Interest rates, 150–151
Internet, 159, 187, 193
Investments, 151–153
Iodine, 53, 57, 58

Jade Mountain, 51, 79, 103, 114, 117, 161

Kelly, Edward, 144
Kerosene, 91–92
    lanterns, 109–110
    stoves, 98–99
Kitchen supplies & equipment, 35–37
Kitchen sundries checklist, 172–173

Lanterns
    battery, 112
    duel-fuel, 107–108
    gas, 106–111
Lead, 49
Levitt Jr., Arthur, 144
Light sticks, chemical, 118
Lighting, 68, 70–72, 106–119, 161, 168
Lighting mistakes, 119
Lindane, 49
Liquidity, 150–151, 152
Loans & mortgages, 140, 153, 154

Medical and dental to-do checklist, 175–176
Medical devices, 128–129
Medical planning, 122–125
Medical records, 123
Mercury, 49
Millet, 12–13
Money, 144–148, 151–153
Morella, Representative Connie, 62
Moving, 163–164
MREs (meals ready to eat), 6–7, 9, 22–24
    advantages/disadvantages of, 23–24

shelf life, 23
storage of, 34
Mutual funds, 149
Mylar bags, 33

Neighborhood watch plan, 161
New York Stock Exchange, 149
Nonprescriptive supplies checklist, 176–177
Nuclear power, 65
Nuclear Regulatory Commission (NRC), 65, 191
Nutrition, 5, 18
Nutritional planning, 29

Off-the-shelf groceries, 6–7, 8, 10–18, 25–26, 34
Oil, 64
Oil lamps, 86

Personal and family hygiene checklist, 176
Pets, 17–18
Pharmaceutical drugs, 123
Police, 67
Polyethylene laminate pouches, 33
Powdered eggs, 15, 28
Powdered milk, 12, 18, 28
Power grid, 64–65, 66, 160
Power outages, *see computers*
Potts, Michael, (*The Independent Home*), 85–86
Prescriptions, 123
President's Council on Year 2000 Conversion, 146
Propane, 89–91
    compared to kerosene, 100
    compared to liquid fuel, 108
    lanterns, 109
    refrigerators, 104–105
    stoves, 97–98
    tank, 164
PŪR Company, 55–56

Radio, 76, 159
Railway system, breakdown of, 3, 64, 158
Real Goods, 114, 184
Recession
  global, 4
  national, 147
Red Cross, 3, 50, 124, 189
Refrigeration, 94, 104–105
Rice, 13

S & P Index, 149
Safe, 143
Sanitation, 47, 138–139
Sanitation and refuse checklist, 178
Securities and Exchange Commission, 144, 191, 192
Security, home, 162–163
Snacks & treats, 15–16
Solar energy, 84–86, 161
  flashlights, 116–117
  recharging batteries, 79, 82–83
  solar ovens, 94, 103–104
  solar radios, 159
Solid fuel, 101–102
Spike dates, 191–192
Spikes (electrical), 67
Sprouting, 14, 30
Stocks & stock market, 146, 148–153
Suppliers, 182–185
Supply & delivery problems, 3

Tanoue, Donna, 146
Telecommunications, 65, 146, 160
Television, 76, 162, 164
Thermoelectric cooler, 105
Tools, 162
Tools checklist, 179–180
Trade/barter system, 154
Transportation, 157–158
Trucking industry, 64
TVP (textured vegetable protein), 21

U.S. Environmental Protection Agency
  water contaminant chart, 48–49
U.S. Senate Y2K Task Force, 3
U.S. Treasury, 151
USDA, 10
Utilities, 65, 154, 155

Vitamins, 16, 130–133

Washing, 137
Water consumption requirements, 41
Water contaminants, see water supply
Water contamination chart, 48–49
Water filters & purifiers, 50–57
  clean water chart, 56–57
  General Ecology purifiers, 53–54
  Katadyn filters, 52–53
  PŪR filters, 55–56
Water preparedness charts, 43, 45
Water preparation checklist, 173
Water storage, 41–45
Water supply
  contaminants, 48, 50, 58, 166
  delivery of, 40, 46, 59
  treatment systems/plants, 39, 40, 45, 47
  Y2K affect on, 40, 146, 166
Water sources, 59–61
Water treatment, 41, 45, 46–59, 61
  boiling, 58–59
  chemical treatment, 55, 57–58
  how to treat, 50–59
Weatherizing, 69–70
Web site resources, 187–190
Woodstoves, 86, 88, 93, 138, 163, 167

Y2K wallop, 146–148
Y2K, profiting from, 151–153
Yardeni, Ed, 146, 149, 190
Yourdon, Edward, 65, 66

ABOUT THE AUTHOR

As a how-to educator, writer, and television producer, Avian Rogers has produced several instructional videos on various aspects of the Year 2000 computer rollover (Y2K) problem with leading experts in the Y2K field, including "Ed Yourdon's Year 2000 Home Preparation Guide" video. In addition to writing and producing this program, she has written and/or appeared in numerous informative programs including PBS's *Hometime*, ABC's *The Home Show*, Lifetime's *Motherworks*, HGTV's *Today at Home*, *The Fix*, and *Country at Home*.

Ms. Rogers was one of the first and youngest female general building contractors in California and so is well-versed in the hands-on requirements of self-sufficiency. Since her earliest adult years living on 120 acres in Northern California without electricity or telephone, self-reliance has always been a cornerstone of her personal life philosophy. Some of her fondest memories are of barn raisings with only hand tools to ease the work, splitting logs to stoke the woodstove, and gathering with friends for fresh baked bread and dinner under the light of kerosene lanterns.

Y2K is something she has been preparing for her whole life.